New Nations and Peoples

Indonesia

Indonesia

LESLIE PALMIER

with 92 illustrations and 3 maps

47268

New York
WALKER AND COMPANY

991
P185i

© Thames and Hudson 1965

All rights reserved. No portion of this work may be reproduced without permission except for brief passages for the purpose of review

Library of Congress Catalog Card Number: 65–22142

First published in the United States of America in 1966 by Walker and Company, a division of Publications Development Corporation

Printed in Great Britain by Jarrold and Sons Ltd, Norwich

To remember my mother

Contents

1   Indonesians and their Land

Peoples

INDONESIANS ARE OF MANY DIVERSE STRANDS. Their islands lie between Asia and Australia, and between South and East Asia. During the course of history, therefore, many peoples have moved in from the Asian mainland. The earliest migrants appear to have been akin to the Melanesian peoples of our day. (One of the oldest fossils of early man was found in Java, but he was not among the ancestors of present-day Indonesians.) The next wave of new-comers (and it must be remembered that these population move- ments lasted several centuries) were a Negrito race still to be found, though rarely, in Africa, South Asia, and Oceania. The culture of both these early invaders may be described as Mesolithic. The original inhabitants on the coast were killed or absorbed, or they fled inland; those in the interior, where life was harder, generally managed to avoid being molested. This sequence of events was to be repeated with every new arrival in the archipelago, so that each of the many islands, although different from the others, is also marked by a sharp distinction between the peoples on the coast and those inland.

More recent arrivals are supposed to have come from southern China, the area roughly covered by the present province of Yunnan, whence they moved to Indo-China and Thailand and so into the archipelago. They came about 3000 B.C. and their migration con- tinued, perhaps in several waves, until the beginning of the Christian era. At first they used Neolithic tools, but towards the end of their migration introduced iron; bronze tools and weapons appear to have been unknown to them. Good sailors, they spread from Madagascar to the farthest eastern islands in the Pacific, and were the ancestors of the present-day Malay-Polynesians. The languages of this group, called Austronesian, include most of the approximately 170 spoken in Indonesia. They may be subdivided into two broad sections; first, the languages of the interior, spoken by the Atjehnese and peoples of the interior of Sumatra, Borneo, and Celebes; second, the languages of the Batak of Sumatra, the Malays on the coasts of Sumatra and Borneo, the inhabitants of Java, and of Bali. The latter languages are closely related to each other and to the Malagassi of Madagascar and the Tagalog of Luzon. It seems probable that the second group of languages came into the archipelago much later than the first. Although Malay is only one of the many languages spoken in the archipelago, it happened to be spoken in the Malay Peninsula and eastern Sumatra. With the intensification of trade, the ports of that region became the meeting-place of people from all the islands, and so made Malay the archipelago's lingua franca, of which modern Indonesian is a variant.

Although most of the languages spoken belong to a common family, nevertheless a person brought up speaking one of them often does not understand another. Linguistic affinity does not imply mutual intelligibility. And as a result of this long-continued migration of people, not only are very many languages spoken in the archipelago, but often several languages are in use on one small island. There is not one, in fact, whose population is not racially mixed; and on all the large islands, except Java, primitive tribes live side by side with much more advanced peoples. This sometimes coincides with the distinction between the coastal peoples and those of the interior.

The Malay immigrants brought with them a highly developed form of agriculture, including the cultivation of rice in irrigated fields; they applied this technique wherever soil and climate were favourable, above all in Central Java. Elsewhere, they grew rice in clearings made by burning the forest. This method is much less productive and requires less organization than the other. So that in the areas where the irrigated method is common, such as in Java, the population is much denser, and the people are organized more hierarchically than in other parts of the archipelago.

The 1961 census found the population to be nearly 96 millions and growing at the rate of 2·3 per cent per annum, so that it probably reached the 100 million mark in 1963.

POPULATION DISTRIBUTION AND DENSITY

	000's	Density per sq. m.
Java (with Madura)	62,700	1,216
Sumatra	15,400	80
Bali and Lesser Sundas	5,500	190
Kalimantan (Borneo)	4,100	19
Sulawesi (Celebes)	6,600	90
Moluccas and West Irian (New Guinea)	1,600	—
TOTAL POPULATION	95,900	129

The 1930 census, which recorded the population by ethnic groups, remains our principal source of information on this important topic. The following table shows the relevant percentages at that time. The 1961 census did not, apparently, inquire into this matter, but no great change seems to have occurred. The people of Java (including Javanese, Sundanese, and Madurese) amounted to 67 per cent of the total population in 1930; they accounted for 66 per cent in 1961.

	per cent
Javanese (Central and East Java)	45
Sundanese (West Java)	14
Madurese (East Java and Madura)	8
Coastal Malays (Central Sumatra and Borneo)	8
Makassarese-Buginese	4
Menangkabau (Central Sumatra)	3
Balinese	2
Batak (North Sumatra)	2
Atjehnese (North Sumatra)	1
	—
TOTAL	87
	—

Islands

Indonesia is the largest country in Southeast Asia. Its 3,000 islands cover a distance of some 3,200 miles. This is roughly as far as from the west of Ireland to the Caspian Sea; or from the west coast of the United States to Bermuda in the Atlantic; or from Perth in Western Australia to Wellington in New Zealand. The archipelago lies in an arc ('a garland of emeralds flung around the equator' was how a rhapsodical Dutch writer described it) between Australia and the Asian mainland (specifically, between 5° N. and 10° S., and between 95° and 140° E.). Its land area totals some 735,000 square miles (including Western New Guinea) or about a quarter that of the United States, and about eight times that of Britain. The five largest islands in the archipelago are Java, Borneo (the northwestern part of which is in Malaysia), Sumatra, Celebes, and New Guinea, of which the eastern half is Australian.

Being on the Equator, most of the country is hot throughout the year, though not excessively so, and enjoys little variation. At Djakarta, the capital, for example, the highest temperature recorded is 96° F., and the annual range of average monthly temperatures is a matter of only two or three degrees. High elevations enjoy a cooler temperature. The yearly average at Bandung, 2,200 feet above sea-level, is 72° F.; at Djakarta, close to sea-level, it is 79° F. These differences are reflected in the natural vegetation and the crops on mountain slopes; tea gardens, for example, follow contour lines.

Rainfall throughout most of the country distributes itself into two seasons: the wet and the dry. In Djakarta the average annual rainfall is 80 inches; the August average is 2 inches, the January 12 inches. The coming of the wet season is often unpredictable; it may be late or may be very marked, and crops may be severely damaged by drought or flood.

Differences in rainfall, which ranges from some 20 inches in protected valleys to over 300 inches on exposed mountain slopes, are matched by variations in vegetation. Where the dry season is truly so, savannah grasses and monsoon forests are found; in areas of heavy rainfall with no long dry season, luxurious tropical forests predominate.

12

The density of population is closely related to the fertility of the soil. Only western Sumatra, the Lesser Sunda islands, and especially Java, have soils which can support large numbers. Much of this land is hilly, and over the centuries the peasantry have harnessed the fertility of the soils by terracing the hill-sides. Some of these areas have densities as high as 3,000 to 4,000 people to the square mile; Java has over 1,200. But Borneo, for example, the world's largest island after Greenland, has less than 50 people per square mile. So also with the smaller islands; some are virtually uninhabited, others, such as Bali, are intensively cultivated.

Though all the islands of the Indies differ in very many respects, the great division is between Java (usually taken to include the small island of Madura on its northeast coast) and the others. Long before the coming of the Dutch, Java's exceptional fertility had made it the rice-bowl of the archipelago. It was here, too, that the Dutch established themselves most firmly and introduced important estate crops such as coffee, tea, quinine, rubber, and coconut palms, whilst inducing the peasantry to grow sugar-cane and tobacco. With law and order secured, and the later introduction of hygienic measures, the population of Java increased rapidly. In 1815 it was thought to amount to some 5 millions; in 1961, as the table on page 11 shows, it had risen to 63 million. The consequence is that now it requires imports of rice to subsist, and the cash crops it produces are not enough to pay for them. In other words, whereas it had supplied the other islands with food, now Java depends on them for it. As we shall see, this situation has led to political trouble.

Development in the other islands of the archipelago, while not as intensive as Java, has nevertheless been significant. The spice trade was based on the Moluccas, but its importance declined with the passage of time. Tobacco and rubber have been grown in north-eastern Sumatra, and oil-fields developed in Sumatra and Borneo. Bauxite deposits in the islands of the Riau archipelago near Singapore have been exploited recently, and tin has been mined on the islands of Bangka and Billiton off southeastern Sumatra. The peoples of these islands are in consequence the major earners of foreign exchange.

2 Indian Influences

Hindu-Buddhism

TWO THOUSAND YEARS AGO the people of the Indonesian islands still lived in small communities, relatively democratic in character, devoted to rice-growing or fishing. Though in many tribes and even races, their level of culture was probably similar everywhere. Their religious beliefs were primitive, and featured the worship of ancestors. They have left behind them small stone pyramids, which appear to have been constructed at about the time that iron tools and weapons were introduced. These constructions remained sacred for later religions, in some cases continuing as places of worship down to our own day.

It is supposed that even at that early date traders travelled between the east coast of India and Indonesia, and between Indonesia and what is now Vietnam. Nevertheless, Indonesians knew little of the outside world, and the outside world little of Indonesia. The first Western author to write about Indonesia was the Greek geographer Ptolemy of Alexandria (A.D. 160). A passage in the Hindu epic the *Ramayana*, inserted at about the same period, also mentions Indonesia (as *Yavadvipa*), and described it as having seven kingdoms. It would therefore seem that even at this early date there were organized Indonesian communities. However, these were not states properly speaking, but rather consisted of rulers exerting some kind of personal authority over a vaguely defined area and a number of settlements.

These kingdoms were given a much firmer structure by Indian civilization, which appears to have started infiltrating into the islands in the third century A.D. What Indianized the archipelago, in so far

14

as this took place, is still uncertain. The most plausible theory is that certain rulers, either deliberately or by accident, acquired the services of Hindu Brahmins and so considerably increased their power; other monarchs, to keep their end up, did the same. It must be remembered that Brahmins, like other priests in similar cultures, were the repositories not only of religious knowledge, but also of much lore concerning economic activity. For example, only they could tell, by means of occult, the best times to plant or to harvest. Most of these Brahmins came from a kingdom, famous in those days, on the coast of Coromandel; but all the coastal areas of India may well have contributed to the expansion of its culture.

Similarly, in our day, states obtain the services of technicians either from the Western powers or from the communists; some, of course, from both. Then, just as some of the fiercest protagonists of modern methods in the poorer countries are their own nationals, so also it is possible that some of the 'Hindus' in these early states were actually people from the archipelago who had acquired Brahminical lore in India and returned to apply their knowledge in their homelands.

The above is to a considerable extent speculation; all we know for certain is that a number of Indonesian principalities existed in the fifth, sixth, and seventh centuries; that some of them may have already existed in the second century, and that they may have been situated anywhere in the archipelago except in the Moluccas and the more eastern of the Lesser Sunda islands. Their rulers drew ideological sustenance from India, but carried on a little trade with both India and China. It also appears probable that some of these monarchies accepted Buddhism in and after the fifth century. They did not reject Hinduism to do so, but added Buddhism to it. A few words about these religions seem to be in order.

Hinduism and Buddhism are both offsprings of Brahmanism, the religious and social system of the Aryans who invaded India from Iran in about 1500 B.C. It placed great importance on the correct performance of sacrifice by the priests; even the deities being made dependent upon it. This sanctioned, and may have reflected, the power of the priests, who, like the social and physical scientists of today, were thought capable of ensuring happiness, wealth, and power, and controlling the forces of nature. In addition, their position was protected by a system whereby the population was divided into four groups, each with its own customs, laws, rights, and obligations. Only Aryans belonged to the three highest, and the Brahmins were at the top. This caste system has remained distinctive of India.

The Aryans originally worshipped deities which were personifications of natural phenomena; these in due course gave way to Brahman, the One, Unchanged, and Attributeless Being. From speculation as to the relation between the self and the divine, there developed the doctrine of the transmigration of souls (*samsara*), which forms the nucleus of both the Hindu and the Buddhist outlook on life and the world. Each new self is conditioned by *karma*, the deeds and thoughts of the self in the preceding incarnation.

In due course a reaction against the power of the priests occurred, and a number of sects emerged contesting the meaning of the sacrificial ritual and rejecting the authority of the priests. Two developed into independent religions: Jainism and Buddhism. Jainism has had no influence in the archipelago, so may be disregarded. Buddhism, however, has strongly affected Indonesian life.

Siddharta Gautama, who later took the name of Buddha, the Enlightened One, was born in 563 B.C., the son of a minor prince. As a young man he fled his palace, driven by a yearning to find true mysticism. In a famous sermon at Benares, he enunciated the fundamentals of his doctrine. Life itself is sorrow, which is the consequence of desire, and this results from ignorance. To achieve salvation, one must gain knowledge. Desire is then eliminated, and the cycle of causation which leads from one life to another is interrupted. *Nirvana* (literally extinction) is then attained.

Gautama taught that salvation can be found by each individual; he therefore rejected the need for priests. In this, his doctrine was similar to that of the much later Protestant Reformation within Christianity in Europe. Gautama preached his message during the course of wanderings throughout northwest India, and by the time of his death in 480 B.C. he had a large number of disciples.

As time passed, Buddha began to be regarded as a supernatural being, and Buddhism divided into two main streams, *Hinayana* (Lesser Vehicle), also called *Theravada* (of the elders); and *Mahayana* (Greater Vehicle). Hinayana concentrates upon personal salvation, its ideal being other-worldly monasticism. It did not spread to Indonesia, which was strongly affected by Mahayana. This teaches that one obtains salvation in order to confer it upon other beings. Those who have attained salvation *bodhi*, and stand on the threshold of *nirvana*, but who renounce it in favour of other beings, are called *Bodhisattvas*. In this sense everybody can become one here on earth.

Mahayanism also taught that Gautama was only *one* in a long series of Buddhas from previous aeons (the process of creation was divided into aeons). These terrestrial Buddhas, however, were regarded merely as reflections of celestial Buddhas, called Dhyani Buddhas, who were seated on lotus flowers, absorbed in meditation, inactive and in the highest state of tranquillity.

The appearances of each individual terrestrial Buddha were separated by thousands of years. In between, man was assisted by celestial Bodhisattvas who emanated from rays of light sent to earth by the Dhyani Buddhas. This belief in Bodhisattvas inspired Buddhist art deeply wherever Mahayana prevailed. Inevitably, Mahayana evolved into a polytheism, and only too easily came under the influence of other religions. Popular gods were accepted in between the celestial Bodhisattvas, and the original doctrine of salvation receded ever further into the background. It also incorporated ancient magic conceptions. The early Bodhisattvas became magicians who could impose their will even upon gods, spirits, and demons with the aid of supernatural powers; they were also thought capable of attaining salvation at any given moment. This version of Buddhism came to be known as Tantrism and at a certain period was quite influential in Java. Mahayana's acceptance of local gods and beliefs, however, may well have been the reason why it spread so far; from India to Tibet, to Southeast Asia, to China, and to Japan.

Hinduism was in a sense a 'counter-reformation' against Buddhism and Jainism; in due course it extirpated the former from India. Like Mahayana Buddhism, it accepted the local gods, who were given a recognized place, and so a pantheon came into existence with new rites and ceremonies. These deities were regarded as manifestations of a supreme god, no longer just tools of the priests.

The Hindu theologians regarded Brahman as manifest in three gods: Brahma, Creator of the world; Vishnu, Guardian of the world; and Shiva, Destroyer of the world. The faithful, however, worshipped either Vishnu or Shiva. Vishnuism placed emphasis on service and love of god; Shivaism had rather an ascetic bias.

Shiva's mystical consort is a goddess, *Shakti*, who personifies divine power. She appears in various manifestations, such as Durga, Kali, Parvati, and others. In the Shiva cult other gods also appear who are believed to be manifestations of Shiva himself, or sons of a union between him and Durga. One of them is Ganesha, who takes the form of an elephant, and is the protector of learning. In Shivaism the union of the transcendental and the immanent world is brought about through the sexual union of Shiva and Durga interpreted in mystical fashion. Hence the cult has a strong sexual note, and its emblem is the phallus, *linga*.

Those who believe in Vishnu, however, see their god personified in many creatures, such as fish or tortoises, and in figures such as Krishna, Rama, and others. One of the two great Indian epics, the *Ramayana*, tells the story of Rama's life; the other, the *Mahabharata*, portrays Krishna. Historical personages too may be regarded as incarnations of Vishnu; this often occurred in Java.

Representations of Shiva and Vishnu, and their accompanying Shaktis, are frequently found in plastic art, especially in Java. So also are their mounts: for Shiva, a bull, *Nandi*; for Vishnu, a celestial eagle, *Garuda*; and for Brahma a goose, *Hamsa*. The Garuda is now the Indonesian national symbol. Incarnations of Vishnu, as well as of many other gods and demons, are also represented.

Since both Mahayana Buddhism and Hinduism enshrined the doctrine of *samsara* and developed into polytheisms, the ground was laid for the fusion which later occurred in Southeast Asia. The social conditions here were unlike those in India, where Hinduism and Buddhism were irreconcilable enemies; in Southeast Asia the two religions (or more accurately their priesthoods) lived in peace.

By the seventh century the most important island in the archipelago was Sumatra, which was divided into two kingdoms. The northern was named Malayu, with its capital on the present site of Jambi. The southern, with its capital at Palembang, was Shrivijaya. In time Shrivijaya became the great sea-based power of western Indonesia, and boasted a flourishing centre of Buddhist theology and philosophy. Java had one kingdom in Central Java, another in East Java, while a third may have existed in West Java.

Both Java and Sumatra developed rapidly in the eighth century. But whereas there are no monuments dating from this period at Sumatra, there are many at Java. Among them are those of the Dieng plateau, nearly 6,000 feet above sea-level. These are temples, whose art is mainly Hindu, dedicated to Shiva.

Shortly after the erection of these monuments, however, a great change must have occurred. In the last quarter of the eighth century and the first half of the ninth, Central Java came under the control of a Buddhist dynasty, the Shailendra. They ruled both Java and Sumatra, and were the most powerful dynasty in Southeast Asia. Control, in those days, meant only the exercise of authority over the more densely settled areas and those important for sea trade, which provided the ruler's income. Many people were so remote from the centre of power, however, that they probably knew and cared little about the current ruler.

Under the Shailendras the Borobudur, the greatest of all Indonesian monuments, was built. It covers the upper part of a hill which has been shaped into a series of terraces, while the floors and the walls retaining the terraces have been faced with stone. The top of the hill has been flattened and made to look like the roof of an enormous building. In the centre of this roof there is a well-shaped *stupa*, or burial mound containing, or believed to contain, a statue of Buddha. Around it there are numerous smaller stupas of stone fretwork which contain statues of the Dhyani Buddhas. The walls of the terraces are covered with some 1,400 sculptures. Each set of reliefs illustrates a story related to Buddhist tradition, so that they amount to a textbook in stone of Mahayana doctrine.

At about A.D. 860, however, the Shailendras lost control of

Central Java to a Shivaist dynasty from East Java called Mataram and withdrew to Sumatra. The new dynasty left its mark in a complex of temple ruins at Prambanan, on the boundary between the present-day districts of Jogyakarta and Surakarta. It contained three large temples dedicated to the Brahmanic trinity: Vishnu, Shiva, and Brahma. These were decorated with sculptured works depicting scenes from the *Ramayana*. The whole temple complex may have been a mausoleum; with the king entombed in the main temple, and the dignitaries of empire in the smaller ones dedicated to the specific gods who protected the various districts of the state.

These monuments were built at the beginning of the tenth century, not more than forty years after the Shailendras disappeared from Java, and near their deserted palace. This does not mean that there had been a violent revolution against them. It is more likely that with the decline of their power a new specific to cure political ills was sought in a return to Shivaism. Because it was officially espoused, however, did not mean that the people were compelled to follow suit. The situation in contemporary Poland, where the official doctrine is of atheistic communism, but where the people follow the Catholic faith with little, if any, hindrance, suggests a parallel.

The centre of power in Java next shifted to East Java, for reasons still unknown. One plausible theory suggests that the building of the Borobudur bore so heavily on the peasantry that they moved eastwards, out of the grasp of the Central Javanese rulers, into the then relatively empty but fertile lands of East Java. The translation may also have been the result of the silting up of Semarang harbour, or of violent volcanic activity. However it may be, East Java became predominant in the island and, incidentally, for the first time Bali begins to assume prominence.

In Sumatra, Shrivijaya under the Shailendras waxed in strength and continued loyal to Mahayana Buddhism. It remained much more in contact with the outside world, and one of its rulers founded an institution at the Buddhist 'university' of Nalanda in Bengal. Another ordered a temple to be constructed at Nagapatam in the territory of the powerful Indian rulers of Chola on the coast of Coromandel (Cholamandala). But in 1025 a Chola ruler devastated

Shrivijaya, went on to do the same to Malayu in the north, and subdued the vassals on the Malay Peninsula. Though it was fatally weakened, Shrivijaya continued to be an important Buddhist centre, as well as the predominant power in the archipelago.

No doubt partly in consequence of the weakening of Shrivijaya, the Mataram dynasty in Java grew stronger. Its greatest ruler, Airlangga, put an end to the rivalry with Shrivijaya and brought the whole of Java under his sway.

Islam

The agents of change first appeared in the twelfth century. Better communications had led to a growth of commerce; and an increasing number of traders came from India to the Indonesian islands, especially to the Moluccas, to buy pepper, spices, and precious wood, or to rest before going on to China. The earlier Indian voyagers had come from Coromandel in the south; these came from Gujarat on the northwest coast. To this area an increasing number of Persian merchants had been coming from the ninth century onwards; by the thirteenth Islam had gained the upper hand. With trade, therefore, the Gujaratis also brought Islam (much influenced by Indian mysticism), though there is nothing to show that they were intent on proselytizing their faith. Marco Polo called at the northeastern coast of Sumatra in 1292, and noted that the inhabitants of a small town (Perlak) on the northern tip of Sumatra had been converted to Islam. It was from there that the religion entered the archipelago.

The first half of the thirteenth century saw the rise of an important kingdom in East Java, Singhasari. Hinduism by now had become wholly Javanese; the distinction between Hinduism and Buddhism had been lost from sight, and Tantrism was dominant. This had been imported from Tibet, and its spread had been fostered by the knowledge that the mighty Emperor of China, Kublai Khan, had been initiated into Tantrist secret knowledge and practices.

Kublai Khan was the grandson of Chingiz Khan, whose empire in 1227 had extended from Russia to the China Sea. Towards the end of the same century his armies repeatedly attacked Japan and the countries of Southeast Asia. Though they alarmed many, they met

SOUTH CHINA
SEA

ATJEHNESE
GAYO=
ALAS
BATAK
NIASSANS
MENANGKABAU
COASTAL
MALAYS
MENTAWEIANS
REDJANG
LAMPONG
GROUP
ENGANESE

PU
IBAN
BAHAU
GROUP
LAND
DYAK
GROUP
NGADJU
GROUP
COASTAL MALAYS
MAKA
-BUC
GR

BADUI
SUNDANESE
JAVANESE
MADURESE
SASA
BALINESE

INDIAN OCEAN

JAVA SEA

SCALE

0   200   400 MLS.

■ KUBU GROUP

Map showing ethnic groups

with little success. However, their expeditionary force into Java, which fulfilled mainly punitive tasks, fortuitously brought to birth the last and greatest Hindu-Javanese kingdom, the empire of Madjapahit.

From this period, too, come the first records of Chinese settlements in Indonesia; formed not by immigrants, but by shipwrecked sailors, pirates, and so forth. Thus the seeds were laid for present-day Indonesian society, an amalgam, though perhaps not a blend, of Western civilization, Indonesian culture, and Chinese enclaves.

Madjapahit's Empire lasted barely a century, from 1293 to 1389. It is principally renowned for the name of one of its prime ministers, Gadjah Mada, who made a large number of the archipelago's petty principalities give their allegiance to his king. One significant exception was Sunda, in West Java, which never submitted.

Both Buddhist and Shivaist rites were followed in Madjapahit, and the priesthoods of both were supported by the state. Their main task was to maintain all the sanctuaries where kings were buried, which it was the king's duty to visit, venerating the gods, satisfying his ancestors, and participating in their magic strength. He travelled with his many followers. They rode on horses and elephants, with vehicles drawn by mules and oxen, while the royal harem and its lone husband journeyed in stately carriages. The villages through which the cortège passed had to provide cattle, rice, and vegetables for the crowd of visitors, and give the king the choice of their virgins.

Few people knew how to read and write, and most of them belonged to the clergy. Their superintendents were high state officials. It was the duty of the clergy to look after the archives; each convent and each temple had its own charters and documents. Gadjah Mada made a general survey of laws and customs. Fixed rules existed for internal government, which was entrusted to some of the close relatives of the king. This system of administration was to continue virtually unchanged into the nineteenth century. The king collected taxes in produce from the villages (the basic social units), not from individuals, and he rewarded his faithful servants by granting them the income of one or more villages, which had to supply food and labour to their lords. In exchange, these villages paid no general taxes. Other villages were given the charge of taking care of sanctuaries and of the priests who served them, and many of these foundations continued to exist until modern times.

The capital of Madjapahit was surrounded by a solid high red-brick wall. The western gate led into a wide plaza, in the middle of which was a deep pool of clean water. Around the plaza were several rows of tall trees; there policemen walked up and down. On the north side of the plaza was the main gate with decorated iron doors, which led to the tournament fields. In the centre of these stood a pavilion for the king; on one side was a hall for audiences and for the meetings of the royal council; on the other was a meeting-place where the Shivaitic and Buddhist priests held discussions and arranged about offerings. When the king came to attend the sacifice, the whole plaza was carpeted with flowers. Around the plaza the royal princes had their quarters; Gadjah Mada had his to the north-east. In the plaza, the king amused himself with the contests and war games of his noblemen. There he invited thousands of his followers to dinner. The buffoons went round, the whole company joined in singing; and the royal family entertained their guests.

Thus was life for the rulers of Madjapahit. With its fall, the capital vanished. It was a characteristic of Indonesian, as of other Asian kingdoms, that the capitals (or *kraton*) were tied to the dynasties; every new dynasty founded a new capital.

We have seen how the formation of political communities on a wider base than that of the tribe was the consequence of the importation of new techniques of communication and control, formally labelled Hindu and Buddhist, from India. Two different types of empire had eventually arisen: Shrivijaya, controlling the shipping lanes; and Madjapahit, organizing the labour power of a relatively compact population. The Hindu-Buddhist techniques of adminis-tration, if so they may be called, however, had proved inadequate to the task of uniting the archipelago. Indeed, until the coming of the Dutch, the history of Java followed a certain repetitive cycle. Wars between principalities were succeeded by a certain measure of order imposed by whoever emerged victorious. In due course the local rulers increased their strength to the point where they could challenge the ruling dynasty. Another period of 'wars of succession' then ensued, with an eventual victor, and so the cycle continued. The means of communication and control were never adequate to maintain peace for any considerable period. Thus, Shrivijaya had collapsed before Madjapahit, whose success in turn was limited to the lifetime of Gadjah Mada. With his death, the empire fell into disarray. The day of Hindu-Buddhism was done; now Islam took over.

How Islam converted the archipelago is almost as much a matter of mystery and controversy as the previous Hinduization many centuries earlier. The vanguard were of course the Muslim traders; they are the main means of expansion of Islam today into the interiors of the more remote islands, where the people are still animists. But the new religion may have been adopted by certain coastal princes as a counter to the threat of Portuguese Christianity; it has been observed that as the Portuguese spread their dominion, so they found the Muslims always just ahead. It is also thought that Muslim proselytizers worked in the countryside to convert the village people, once the official adherence of the princes had been obtained. However it may have been, Islam was adopted peacefully.

The first Islamic state of consequence in the archipelago lay outside present-day Indonesia, in Malacca. A glance at the map (on p. 188) will show how well placed it was to command the sea-routes of the region. Within easy reach of traders from Java and, more important, midway between India and China, it became in a few years the principal port of the islands. It was helped by the rise of the Ming dynasty who overthrew the Mongols in China, began expanding southwards, and shielded Malacca against the T'ai kings.

Though Malacca was not originally Islamic, the fact that most of the traders who called there were Muslims no doubt helped considerably towards its conversion. Then, in the early fifteenth century, Islam spread along the northeast coast of Sumatra, the coastal districts of the Malayan peninsula, and the north coast of Java. Towards the end of that century, following the spice-route, it reached the Moluccas. Its expansion at this time was slow, and not until the middle of the sixteenth century did it pick up speed.

At the beginning of the fifteenth century some of the Javanese coastal principalities were ruled by Muslims, others by Hindu-Buddhists. With the decline of the power of Madjapahit, that of the local rulers increased. The weakening of central control was furthered by the growth of the spice trade consequent on increased demand from Europe. The princes of the coastal States took a share of the profits by bringing spices from the Moluccas and shipping them to Malacca. It is very likely they used Gujarati and Malay traders as their agents, encouraging them to settle in or near their towns. No doubt, it helped matters when the rulers too accepted Islam, as many did, without necessarily abandoning their previous Hindu-Buddhist practices. Madjapahit finally fell before a coalition of Muslim princes between 1513 and 1528, the strongest Javanese power thereafter being the north coast principality of Demak.

1 The people of the Indonesian archipelago are of diverse origins. The ancestors of this man from Central Java were probably Malays who emigrated from the Asian mainland in about 3000 B.C.

2 As a result of this long-continued migration, very many ethnic groups, each with its own language, are to be found in the archipelago. These Balinese women are preparing for market.

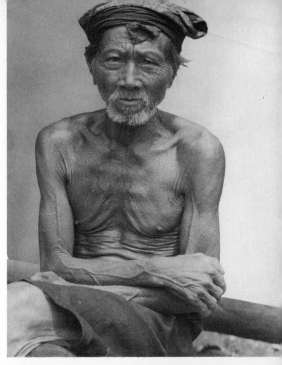

3 The Batak people of Sumatra live in decorated houses like these.

4 In Java most houses are still made of bamboo though some are now built of brick in Western style.

5 The Malay immigrants brought with them a highly developed form of agriculture including the cultivation of rice in irrigated fields. This is one of the many paddy fields in Bali.

6 The coastal people have also been fishermen since very early times. These are from Java.

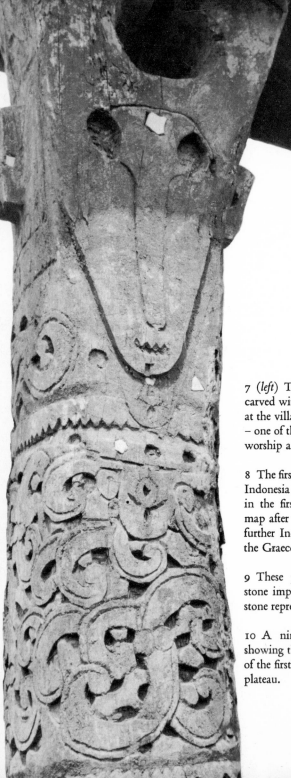

7 *(left)* This wooden post has been carved with the face of a buffalo-man at the village of Mengulewa in Flores – one of the many features of ancestor worship and animistic belief.

8 The first Western author to write of Indonesia was Ptolemy of Alexandria in the first century A.D. This early map after Ptolemy's *Geography* shows further India as it was conceived by the Graeco-Roman world.

9 These people in Flores still use stone implements, and the figures in stone represent their ancestors.

10 A nineteenth-century engraving showing the ruins of a Hindu temple of the first century A.D. on the Dieng plateau.

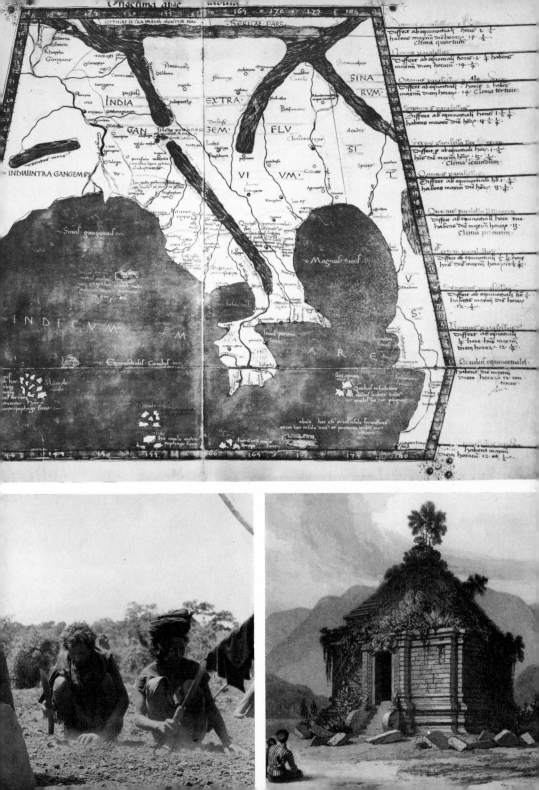

11 Between the first and third centuries A.D., Indian civilization began to infiltrate the archipelago, possibly as a result of contact with Hindu Brahmins. This bronze statuette of the god Brahma, representing the classic Indian tradition, was found on Java.

12 Brahman was regarded as manifest in three gods: Brahma, Vishnu and Shiva. The mount of Shiva, the destroyer of the world, was represented as a bull *Nandi* shown here at Prambanan which dates from the first century A.D.

13 The god Shiva, made in stone and dating from the Madjapahit period of the thirteenth century.

14 The most powerful dynasty in the seventh century was the Shailendra who built the great Buddhist temple at Borobudur. A relief from this temple illustrates a story in the Buddhist tradition.

15 By the time this map was made, in 1576, Muslim traders had appeared and may have been one of the causes of the conversion from Hindu-Buddhism to Islam.

16 Though much of Indonesia converted to Islam, Bali remained outside its influence. This traditional Balinese woodcarving shows Vishnu, Guardian of the world, mounted on *Garuda*, a celestial eagle.

3 European Contenders

Portuguese

ISLAM ITSELF OWES MUCH to Christian and Judaic ideas, so it came in a sense as a precursor of the West in the archipelago. Certainly the Muslims were quickly followed by the Portuguese, who sought the wealth of the spicelands, further encouraged by their crusading zeal against the Moors. Their pathfinder was Vasco da Gama, who reached the coast of India in 1498. But it was Albuquerque who gave the Portuguese their empire in Asia. He took Goa in 1509, and two years later the Muslim stronghold itself, Malacca. The Portuguese then made contact with the Moluccas, with the intention of enforcing a monopoly on the spice trade to Europe. The gains to be had were immense. Magellan, who circumnavigated the world in 1519–22, made the first direct shipment to Europe; on arrival the spices were sold at a profit of 2,500 per cent. However, as Europe's demand then was relatively fixed, to have shipped increasing quantities would only have reduced prices and profits.

The Portuguese set to work by driving their only competitors, the Muslim traders, from the seas. This also fulfilled a religious purpose, as the loss of spices meant less revenue for the Egyptian and Syrian trading cities. These had recently come under the dominion of Turkey, whose fleets the Christians had to fight in the Mediterranean. In much the same convenient way, the rulers of Atjeh, a state of North Sumatra, had extended their power by first accepting the new religion of Islam in the second half of the sixteenth century, then launching a series of 'holy wars' against their neighbours, which gave them control over the pepper-growing areas on Sumatra's north-western coast. Similarly, the Prince of Brunei in North Borneo extended his new-found faith and his rule simultaneously to the northeast, subduing the north coast of Borneo and the Sulu islands.

The fall of Malacca had not destroyed Muslim power in the archipelago. Atjeh was one of its main bastions. The others were Demak, later succeeded by adjacent Japara in Java the main inter-mediate shipping ports of the archipelago); Johore, founded by the ex-sultan of Malacca after his city fell to the Portuguese; and Ternate and its rival Tidore in the Moluccas, who between them controlled a large part of the clove and nutmeg production. All these appear to have been sea-based states, much like Malacca itself, whether Islamic or Portuguese. Though they succeeded in arresting the growth of the power of the Portuguese, these Muslim strongholds never managed to combine sufficiently to expel them. Ternate, indeed, concluded a treaty which secured the monopoly of the clove trade for the Portuguese.

Portugal's position was not to endure; other Europeans were on the way. The Spaniards had first appeared in 1521, when Magellan's ship *Victoria* had passed through the Moluccas. Attempts to pacify them in Europe had no effect, and the Spaniards allied themselves with Tidore, Ternate's rival. Officially at peace, Spain and Portugal then fought under the banners of these two principalities for control of the spice trade. A brief interlude of peace followed on agreement in Europe. But in 1570, in consequence of Portuguese treachery, Ternate revolted; and the Spaniards reappeared the same year, when they founded the city of Manila, and extended their authority farther and farther south. The garrison on Ternate fell in 1574, and Portuguese power went into decline. However, in 1580 Philip II of Spain united Portugal to his throne. This ended all fighting between Spaniards and Portuguese in the Indies, but also invited all Spain's enemies to attack the Portuguese possessions.

After the Spaniards came the Englishmen. Francis Drake passed through in 1579, Cavendish in 1586, others later. But more impor-tant were the Dutch, who first reached Indonesian waters in 1596. They had long been sailing the Atlantic far and wide, but it was the

closing of the port of Lisbon by Philip II, against whom the Nether-
landers were in revolt, that precipitated them eastwards for the spices
they were so denied.

Dutch

The first visit convinced the Dutch that the voyage was profitable,
and an increasing number of ships were sent to the Indies. The
United East India Company was formed in 1602 and received from
the States-General (or Parliament) of the Netherlands a monopoly
for all commerce in Asia. It set about driving the Portuguese out of
Indonesian waters. Its first foothold was the island of Amboina,
which recognized the suzerainty of the Netherlands in 1605. Though
the Dutch attacked Malacca in the next year, they were unsuccessful,
and thirty-five years were to pass before they could capture it.

About this time, too, a new naval power arose at Makassar on the
southwest coast of the Celebes, which up to then had not played
any significant role in Indonesian history. After Portuguese and
Dutch traders had visited this kingdom, the ruler opted for Islam
in 1605.

Demak and Ternate had been exhausted by the struggle against
the Portuguese, and Demak fell under the sway of the rising inland
Javanese Muslim power of Mataram. Only Atjeh emerged with
increased power and reputation. It was on the point of gaining
complete supremacy over the native states of the northwestern archipelago when Portuguese Malacca, Johore, and Patani combined
together in 1629 and crushed it in a great sea battle.

Meanwhile, the Dutch were trading with the various states in
Sumatra. Although these were weak they provided no opportunity
for an extension of Dutch control. Matters were otherwise at the
other end of the archipelago. As the least evil compared with the
Spaniards and Portuguese, Ternate chose the Dutch and they became
the dominant power in the Moluccas. They nevertheless had to reckon
with Makassar, which remained a stronghold of international trade,
dealing with Portuguese, Dutch, English, and Danes, until 1667.

The destinies of the archipelago were, however, to be decided by
the fate of Java. There, the wars of succession had continued.

Mataram had succeeded in absorbing most of the other principalities on the east of the island, as well as Madura, and had even managed to extend its power to Borneo. The only opposition in the east came from a tiny state called Balambangan; but it was strongly supported by the Balinese, who were determined to resist Mataram. This, incidentally, made them hold on to their own Hindu-Buddhism more tenaciously than ever. In the west, however, Mataram was faced by a much more serious opponent, the important port-state of Bantam, also Muslim, which controlled the Sunda lands of West Java. In contrast, Mataram was purely agrarian in character; it had feared and despised the coastal merchant-kings who, weakened by the Portuguese, had proved easy meat.

To secure hegemony over the island, Mataram proposed to attack Bantam. But it had destroyed the basis for any sea power of its own and a land attack was difficult, especially since the Dutch now lay across the main route to Bantam. Their situation in the archipelago, however, was precarious. The Moluccas were grumbling against Dutch claims to monopoly; in Bantam, competition between Dutch, English, and Chinese buyers had sent the price of pepper soaring; at Japara, the Dutch trading post had been destroyed. A saviour was needed, and he duly appeared. In 1618 the United East India Company appointed as Governor-General an ambitious, cruel, and unscrupulous man, Jan Pieterszoon Coen, then aged thirty-one. Coen had sailed to Indonesia first in 1607. During his second tour in 1612 he produced a plan to improve the Company's fortunes; his appointment as Governor-General indicated its adoption.

In essence, Coen intended to widen the Dutch sphere of operations to Asia as a whole, not to restrict it to the archipelago, and to reduce the amount of Company shipping between Asia and Europe. He proposed to plant Dutch settlements in the spice-producing islands, as well as to set up fortified posts in important ports. In addition, he meant to drive the Spaniards from the Philippines and the Portuguese from Macao, and to annihilate all Asian and foreign European shipping. With all competitors to the Dutch removed, the products of Asia would be exchanged for the produce of the spice islands, under the exclusive supervision of Company officials. The profits of this commerce, centred on Batavia, would be sufficient to provide for the quantities of spices and pepper that had to be exported to Europe. While Dutch ships would be busily engaged in trading along the coast of Asia from Persia to Japan, the cargoes to Europe would be only a very few, but they would be worth a king's ransom. He realized that the Company would never make money by trading European commodities for Asian for, as he said, the 'countries of Asia exceed those of Europe in population, consumption of goods, and industry'.[1] It was, in other words, Europe which in relation to Asia was undeveloped, and produced little that Asia wanted. Oddly enough, however, Coen never drew the obvious conclusion that his Dutch settlers would not be able to compete with the Asian traders. What must be strongly emphasized is that Coen had no intention of acquiring political control over the territories in which he intended to plant his settlements. His sole interest was in the network of sea-routes, based on Batavia.

On his appointment as Governor-General, he proceeded to put his plan into effect. He drove the English from the Indies, and they withdrew to India. He then attacked and burnt the town of Jakatra in 1619, and on its site founded the city of Batavia. He blockaded Bantam, and with the English out of the way obtained mastery of the Java sea. To acquire control of the nutmeg trade, he nearly exterminated the population of the Banda islands.

In 1629 Mataram mounted a heavy attack against Batavia. How-ever, it could not provision its armies by overland routes, and Coen continuously attacked its supply ships. In consequence, Mataram's great army was defeated by famine, and withdrew. Bantam, sensing the threat from Mataram greater than that from Batavia (indeed, Mataram saw Batavia merely as an obstacle to its conquest of Bantam), allied itself with the latter. Coen himself died of cholera before victory became clear.

Batavia now emerged as a centre of power in the archipelago. But there were others. On Java itself, Mataram and Bantam were still sovereign, as were Atjeh in Sumatra and Makassar in the Celebes. Spain still held Tidore and Portugal Malacca, but since they were far inferior to the Dutch in sea power, their days were numbered.

4 Unintended Empire

Territorial Dominion

COEN'S GRAND DESIGN became reality by the middle of the
seventeenth century, at the end of the Governor-Generalship of
Anthony van Diemen. Malacca fell to the Dutch in 1641, the
Company became master of the Indonesian seas, and the Dutch
commercial empire reached its zenith. Sixty years after their arrival
in the Indies, years of continuous warfare as well as trade, the Dutch
had achieved their main objects in Asia. Operating exclusively from
sea-bases (Coen's idea of colonists had been abandoned), the Company was controller of the shipping lanes from the Bay of Bengal and
Ceylon to Japan. It had sovereignty over a few places in the Indonesian archipelago of which Batavia was the most important; it also
held Formosa and most of Ceylon. It maintained scores of trading
posts from Ispahan in Persia to Nagasaki in Japan, and in 1652
founded a relay station at the southern point of Africa, the future
Capetown. Cinnamon and cloth from India; copper from Japan
and spices from the Moluccas; silks from Persia and sugar from
China; all were exchanged in Batavia, and only there.

In pursuit of their aims the Dutch were quite ruthless. Just as
Coen had virtually eliminated the people of Banda to maintain a
monopoly of the trade in spices, so his successors reduced the people
of the Moluccas to misery, ruin, and bondage for the same reason.
After 1630, when British competition had been removed, the
Company's profits increased tremendously. They permitted voyages
of navigation from Batavia, which led to Abel Tasman's discovery
of Tasmania and New Zealand.

The Company's establishment of naval supremacy led to its acquisition of territorial dominion. Between 1650 and 1680 all the Indonesian states of importance disintegrated and fell under the Company's sway. Prior to this time there had been no single power strong enough to end their continuous internal struggles; now there was the Company. For its part, convinced that the Portuguese empire had failed because it had been too extensive, the Company was content with control of the shipping lanes and generally shunned the idea of acquiring territorial dominion. So it followed the policy of recognizing any ruler who actually held power and was prepared to meet his obligations to the Company. Nevertheless, circumstances compelled it to acquire territory to protect its commercial empire.

The struggles for succession in the Indonesian states involved such high stakes – winner take all, loser lose all – that the participants often turned to the Dutch rather than risk defeat. (Here as in other parts of Asia, if a handful of Europeans acquired dominion over millions of Asians, it was because enough Asians were on their side. The error is in thinking that Asia is a political term; it is purely geographical.) And if the Company thought that its commercial interests were better safeguarded by supporting one party rather than none, it did so, but imposing such conditions that the peace was not disturbed again, the Company was supreme, and its expenses were recovered. Nor was it averse, on occasion, to stimulating the process.

Makassar, long an outpost of independence from the Company, began to increase its sea power with assistance from British, Danish, and Portuguese traders. The ruler encouraged the Portuguese merchants to trade with the Moluccas. This the Company would not brook, as it claimed a monopoly of trade and shipping. A series of wars ensued, ending in 1667 with the submission of Makassar.

By the next year the native states of the eastern part of the archipelago, from Makassar to the Moluccas, had become vassals of the Company. It had also by this time deliberately crippled Atjeh by fomenting revolt, mainly because the tin-mines of Perak in Malaya, then in a district subject to the Sultans of Atjeh, had aroused its lust. In consequence, control of the coast-lands of Sumatra fell to the Company.

After the fall of Malacca, the only naval power in Asia that could compete with the Company was Turkey in the far west of the continent. In an attempt to court that country, the monarchs of both Bantam and Mataram sent envoys to undertake the pilgrimage to Mecca. Both rulers thereafter assumed the title of Sultan, and adhered more closely to the rules of Islam. One consequence was an elevation in status of the Muslim religious leaders. This led to an abiding tension, not resolved even today, between these, usually commoners by origin, and the traditional aristocracy, which even under the Dutch remained the ruling class down to the middle of the twentieth century, and whose descendants and guiding ideas still play very important roles in Indonesia.

The Company tried for a long time to remain out of Javanese affairs. It had an inflated opinion of Mataram's strength, and underestimated the island's economic value. A state of war with Mataram continued for some time, with sporadic outbursts of violence. Its ruler, Sultan Agung, a few years after his failure to conquer Batavia, moved eastwards and subdued the last Shivaist kingdom of Java, Balambangan. He then tried, but failed, to overwhelm Bali.

When the usual struggle for succession began, the Company's policy initially was one of non-intervention. However, a successful revolt toppled and killed the ruler, and his son offered not only commercial advantages but territory to the Company. The lure was irresistible and Dutch troops were sent to his rescue. They placed him on the throne; as a vassal of the Company, and with a bodyguard of its troops. The Company acquired a large slice of territory south of Batavia as well as the port of Semarang.

Meanwhile, Bantam had been waxing in strength. The ruler of the time devoted himself to modernization and welcomed Europeans: British, Danish, and French. He equipped his own ships which, navigated at first by European captains, sailed to the Philippines, to Macao, to Bengal, and to Persia. He attempted to set up connexions with Turkey, the leading power of Islam. Indian, Chinese, and Arab merchants flocked to Bantam after they were driven out of Malacca and Makassar. Emboldened by his growing strength, the ruler intrigued all over the archipelago against the Dutch. Therefore, when his ambitious son rebelled against him and asked for Dutch help, the Company responded, though virtually the entire Bantamese population sided with the father. Naturally, the prince was put on the throne but, once again, as a Company vassal.

The Company was now supreme in the archipelago; its monopoly system extended over all the islands except Borneo. The Danes left the archipelago altogether. The British, driven from Bantam, built a fortress at Benkulen on the west coast of Sumatra, where they remained for another hundred and fifty years. The Portuguese withdrew to Timor, where they still retain a foothold.

There were now only two protagonists left: the Company and Mataram. They represented, unwittingly perhaps, two very different civilizations. Batavia was the centre of the Company's system. There, a few hundred Dutchmen formed the aristocracy and endeavoured to re-create their way of life. Canals criss-crossed the town, as in Holland, and the houses were placed in close ranks along them. The citadel was built at the seashore, and inside were the residence of the Governor-General, the homes of workmen of the Council, and of those employed at the Arsenal. A large garrison, consisting of more than 1,200 men, paraded every day on a small square in front of the Governor-General's house.

An important part of the Batavia population was Chinese. There were 800 of them in the first year of Batavia's existence; ten years later they had increased to 2,000. They made a living by trade, visiting the small posts and islands that were too unimportant for the Company's ships. They were fishermen and tailors, bricklayers and carpenters; Batavia could not have existed without them. Their chief pastime was gambling. They married Indonesians or bought slave women, and those who returned to China took their sons. Most, however, remained in Batavia all their lives, and educated their sons as Chinese. They lived under their own 'captains', appointed by the Governor-General; later all the inhabitants of Batavia were grouped according to nationality, each under its own chief, also with limited jurisdiction over his subjects.

Mataram, though it had embraced Islam, retained a state structure very similar to that of its Hindu-Buddhist predecessors. The king held a sacral position, as his predecessors had done; and his authority was literally unlimited. Everything and everybody in the kingdom was his property, to be disposed of as he pleased. The highest in the land below the king were the *pangeran*, or princes, either of the ruling royal family or of the royal families of subdued territories; they were all compelled to reside at the court of the king-sultan, to ensure their loyalty and that of their people. The country was divided into a number of districts, each ruled by a governor; the governor of the central district was the king's chief adviser. Two 'commissioners' were appointed, one for the northwest coast and one for the north-east; they were also responsible for foreign affairs. The central part of the kingdom was densely settled. The roads mostly were tracks for horses and pedestrians, and were well guarded; nobody was allowed to leave the central district itself without the sultan's per-mission. The guards also controlled the export of goods.

The king lived in his palace, or *kraton*, a complex network of buildings. Only some of them were open to the public or to foreign ambassadors. Within the palace were kept the sacred heirlooms, hidden from the eyes of the common and unbelieving; on their preservation the safety of the realm was believed to depend. The king appeared in state surrounded only by a bodyguard of women. Even so, he took part in the weekly tournament, and in hunting-parties for which wild beasts were kept in enclosures near the kraton.

However, to return to our story, though Mataram's rulers now owed their thrones to the Dutch, they continued to lay plans to bite the hand that fed them. The Company therefore decided to support a pretender with an avowedly weaker claim. The resulting treaty of 1705 gave the Company complete overlordship of West Java and of the eastern half of Madura. From this date until 1941, the Dutch controlled events in the Indies; and Batavia was the political centre.

Coffee

The conversion of the Company from a sea-trader to a territorial overlord happened conveniently. The policy of developing inter-Asian trade had reached its consummation; after 1693 profits from this source began to fall. The consequences for the Company were masked by an unexpected rise in the European prices for Asian products. It would be wrong to assume, however, that the Company embarked on the new policy because it realized that the old had served its time. Though there were some in the highest councils at Batavia who felt that without a territorial basis the Company's fate was likely to resemble that of the Portuguese, nevertheless the territorial acquisitions were made with an eye exclusively to ensuring either the safety or the monopoly rights of the Company. The Dutch empire is a good example of the unintended consequences of human actions.

The Company might well have found itself with a lot of useless territory acquired to safeguard a commercial system of diminishing profitability but for a fortuitous event: the successful transplantation of the coffee-tree from South India to Java. The story bears some resemblance to the later introduction of the rubber-tree to Malaya: initial failure was followed by overwhelming success. The tree was first planted around 1700, but it was only in 1711 that the first 100 pounds of coffee were delivered to the Company. Nine years later the yearly crop amounted to 100,000 pounds; and twelve years later to 12 millions.

Cultivation of new export crops was quite foreign to the Company's ideas. It wanted a limited supply of Asian products which it could sell at high prices; to this end, it controlled production and maintained a monopoly. The large amount of coffee produced made control over exports impossible. Furthermore, the Company found that coffee was making rich the native heads, the 'regents' as it termed them. This was considered undesirable as leading to too much independence. The Company also had little reason to increase purchasing power in Java, since Holland had little to sell that the people wanted.

So the Company reduced the price it offered for coffee; restricted the area of plantations, and short-paid the producers. Its money in any case went into the pockets of the local heads, not the peasants. In consequence, the latter refused to cultivate the coffee plant, and for many years the Company could not even obtain the limited quantities it wanted. Its answer was to remember that it was the sovereign ruler in the Preanger area of West Java. It demanded that the tribute previously levied by Mataram be delivered in coffee, or that this be sold to the Company at its own price. The new system was established by the middle of the eighteenth century. Coffee was an article of monopoly; the price was fixed and the annual planting of a certain number of new trees was made compulsory. Its cultivation was in the hands of the regents, who were under the control of the Commissioner for Native Affairs, an official nominated by the Governor-General. Supervisors were appointed to assist the regents organize production and maintain the coffee gardens. From these officials, one may note, the civil service of the later Netherlands Indies developed.

Coffee cultivation tied the regents of West Java to the Company by bonds of mutual interest. They became entirely subject to the will of the Commissioner for Native Affairs, who could reduce them to commoners at a moment's notice. Always spending more than they received, they remained perpetually in his debt. At the end of the century the entire production of coffee was not enough to pay the interest on their loans. However, this system brought one great benefit; it put an end to the petty wars which had ravaged the country in the past.

The Company in Decline

With Makassar, Mataram, and Bantam subject to the Company, the whole of Indonesia came effectively under its sway. By the middle of the eighteenth century few of the Indonesian islands were not interfered with by this dominant power.

In Sumatra, Atjeh's power had declined after the Company broke its control of the pepper trade around 1680. Nevertheless, it remained independent until the beginning of the twentieth century. But every other petty state in Sumatra was a subject, in the sense that the exclusive right to handle its most important crops was held by the Company. However, the monopoly could not be enforced as rigorously as in the east of the archipelago. The British at Benkulen, and the proximity of the Asian continent, prevented that.

Borneo was more backward, in all respects, than Sumatra, and only the sultanate of Bandjarmasin was of any significance; but there, too, the various states were subjects of the Company. It is interesting that a sultanate in northwest Borneo called in Chinese miners to work gold-mines. Their numbers grew, friction ensued, and in 1770 the Chinese revolted. From then until 1855 they lived in semi-independent republics. The gold-mines exhausted, they turned to agriculture, and so formed one of the few foreign rural settlements in Indonesia; and they remained thoroughly Chinese.

In the east the archipelago was, for the first time in a long while, at peace under Dutch rule, but the monopoly system was bringing steady impoverishment. The Company's policy was to reduce the production of spices to one-quarter of that before it took control. In addition, the inhabitants of the Moluccas were compelled to buy all foodstuffs from the Company. Not surprisingly, in one century Amboina lost one-third of its inhabitants; while those of Banda were ruined. When the demand for spices did rise in Europe, the Dutch found not only that the inhabitants of the Moluccas could in no way be induced to increase their production, but also that both the British and the French had succeeded in planting clove and nut-meg trees in their colonies in India; the monopoly no longer existed.

In Java the Company's two subject states were disintegrating rapidly. By the treaty of 1705 Mataram, though remaining politically independent, had become an economic vassal of the Dutch; it was compelled to deliver at a set price any amount of rice that the Company might demand. It was to the latter's interest to maintain such a state of affairs, but this proved impossible. The ruler's position was constantly under attack not only by his own vassals but also by members of his own family. He was seen as the agent of a foreign power, hence not deserving of loyalty. Unfortunately, Batavia would not back him to the hilt; its cheapest course was to maintain peace, rather than to support its allies against its enemies. It did not want a politically unified Java, hence it had not supported its subject overlords in any attempt to curb their vassals; nor did it want a situation of war caused by uprisings, since this might have inter-rupted the deliveries of the rice it needed; even less did it want the peace-loving Javanese peasants to turn into warriors. So it simply tried to prevent all military action. However, this policy did not stop the wars of succession which were endemic in Java. When they broke out, the Company supported its own candidate, but of course charged him with the costs of the war. Quite soon he owed the Dutch more than he could hope to pay.

In return for its support, the Company obtained an ever greater measure of economic vassalage. This, in turn, meant that it had to protect the rulers against their own subjects; while the rulers turned to farming out villages to Chinese, who extorted as much as they could from the people.

The Chinese had been growing in numbers, circumventing the Company's attempts to impose a quota system on immigration. Not all could find lawful employment; many of the others turned to plundering in the districts round the capital. The Dutch there-upon decided to deport all unemployed Chinese to Ceylon and South Africa. These came to believe that they would be fed to the sharks on the way, and a general uprising took place. It was bloodily suppressed in Batavia and in some of the northern and northeastern coastal towns; in others, however, it was supported by the local Javanese rulers. Most of Mataram's vassals revolted, and a pretender was placed on the throne. Chaos ensued, and Batavia again inter-vened to put the 'legitimate' ruler on the throne. The price he had to pay was the surrender to the Company, in 1743, of all the coastal districts on Java's northern coast, as well as Java's eastern corner, and the exclusive control of all seaports of Java. Thereafter Mataram became officially a vassal state of the Dutch. The last act of the tragedy was for the ruler of Mataram, shortly before his death in 1749, to secure the succession of his son by ceding all his lands to the Company. The new ruler received the kingdom from the hands of the Governor-General.

This did not please certain members of the ruler's family; they took to the hills, and successfully waged guerrilla warfare against the combined forces of the Dutch and the ruler. Peace was bought in 1755 only by splitting what was left of Mataram into two states, Surakarta and Jogyakarta. Even then the ruler of Surakarta was forced to cede a portion, the Mangkunegara lands, to another discontented member of his family.

Over in the west of the island, in Bantam, a revolt broke out in

1750 and was crushed only by the Company's intervention. It reinstated the ruler whose misgovernment had been responsible for the outbreak, who of course then became completely dependent on the Dutch.

By 1755, therefore, most of Java's 3½ million people were governed directly by Batavia. There were five small Javanese states (Bantam, Cheribon, Jogyakarta, Surakarta, and the Mangkunegara lands) which were the Company's vassals, with Dutch residents at the courts of their rulers. Wars were not permitted, and Java enjoyed a period of relative peace.

With peace came decline. In the seventeenth century the Company had been embattled but powerful; in the eighteenth century it was dominant but waning. The beginning of the end came with the Franco-British-American War of 1780. The Indies were cut off from the Netherlands, and the Company came near bankruptcy. The peace treaty that ended the war opened the seas of the archipelago to British shipping. The final blow was the French Revolution of 1789; the Dutch Republic was occupied without resistance by French troops in 1795. From then until 1810 the Netherlands was practically a vassal of France. On 1 March 1796 a Committee appointed by the government took over the administration of the Company. Its Charter, expiring on 31 December 1799, was not to be renewed.

17 Proximity has permitted migration between China and Indonesia and Chinese settlements began to develop in the thirteenth century. A nineteenth-century photograph of a Chinese pedlar at Djakarta.

18 Today over 90 per cent of Indonesia's population profess Islam. This is part of the yearly celebration of the Prophet Muhammad's birthday at Jogyakarta in Java.

PLANTA · DA · FORTALEZA ·
DE · MALACA ·

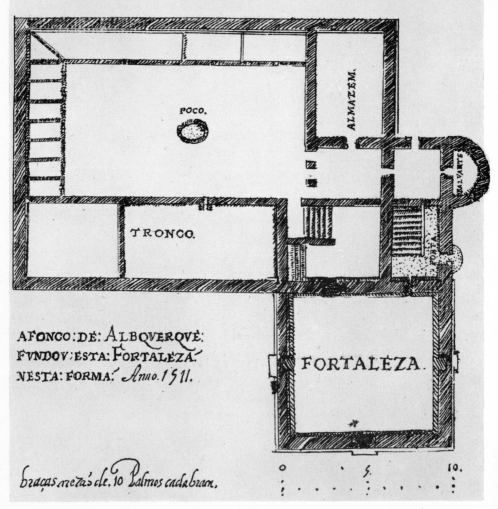

POCO.

ALMAZEM.

BALVARTE

PORTA

TRONCO.

FORTALEZA.

AFONCO : DE : ALBOVERQVE :
FVNDOV : ESTA : FORTALEZA :
NESTA : FORMA : Anno. 1511.

braças metas de 10 Palmos cada bram.

0   5   10.

19 The Muslims were followed by the Portuguese. This is a sixteenth-century drawing of the Portuguese fort at Malacca built by Alfonso d'Albuquerque.

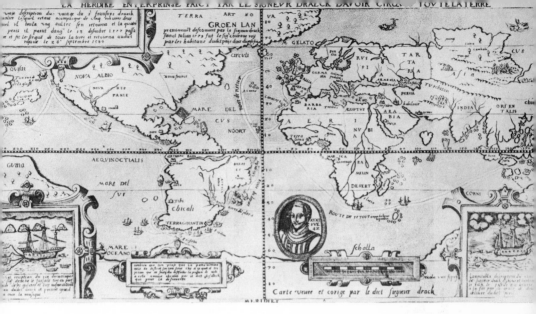

20 Sir Francis Drake passed through Indonesia in 1579. This sixteenth-century map illustrates the route of his voyage.

21 It was the Dutch who finally secured hold of Indonesia. This sixteenth-century engraving shows their trading vessels off the coast of Coromandel in India.

22 The United East India Company, a Dutch mercantile organization, had centred all its activities at Batavia in Java by the beginning of the seventeenth century. A contemporary engraving of the Port of Batavia.

23 A seventeenth-century engraving of the Governor-Generals' palace at Batavia.

24 The first Governor-General of the Company was Jan Pieterszoon Coen (1587-1629) who founded the city of Batavia in 1619.

25 This contemporary engraving illustrates the cruelties inflicted upon the British by the Dutch at Amboina in the course of their struggle for Indonesia.

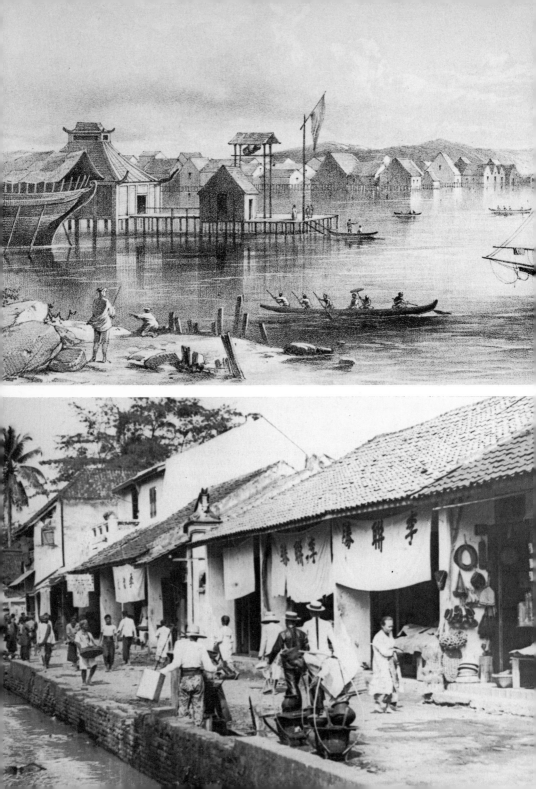

26 The Dutch were also faced with the Javanese Muslim power of Mataram which extended its control as far as Borneo. This is a nineteenth-century engraving of Brunei which was originally under Mataram.

27 (*left below*) When Batavia was founded there were 800 Chinese inhabitants; ten years later the number had increased to 2,000. This is the Chinese quarter at Batavia in the nineteenth century.

28 Batavia was re-named Djakarta when Indonesia became independent in 1944. Today there is still evidence of Dutch influence particularly the canals which criss-cross the town.

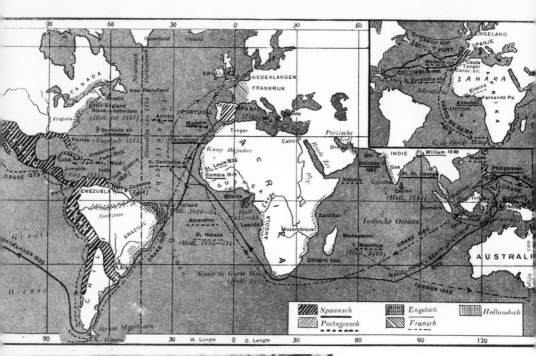

29 This map illustrates the extent of the European trade routes which had developed in the eighteenth and nineteenth centuries.

30 The transplantation of the coffee-tree from South India to Java in the eighteenth century added to the commercial interests of the Company. Coffee has since become a major item of produce. Here the trees are being swept with brooms.

5   The Autocrats

Daendels

BY THE END OF THE EIGHTEENTH CENTURY nearly all the territories in the Indies which had once belonged to the Company, except Java, had been lost to the British. The total garrison of Java itself amounted to only 1,000 European and 2,000 native soldiers. Fortunately, the British were too precariously poised in India to take Java, and limited themselves to sailing round the island, destroying the Company's once powerful navy and its repair wharves.

Paradoxically, this period of great military weakness was also one of sudden wealth. With the links between the Netherlands and the Indies broken, Batavia sold tropical products to all comers at their own risk, at a much greater profit than that of the Company when goods were carried in its own ships. This period, too, was ended by the fortunes of war, which put an abrupt end to visits by Danish and American ships. But ten years of prosperity had put 2 million guilders into the war-chest.

This treasure was soon exhausted by the new Governor-General, Herman Willem Daendels. At one time a small-town lawyer, he had risen on the crest of the revolutionary wave. Arriving with extraordinary powers, he acted as a dictator, and with great energy reformed the administration and eradicated corruption. The Javanese hereditary district rulers were made civil officials and all officials were given military rank. Daendels reformed the system of justice into courts which worked according to Dutch-Indies statutes. Later administrations were to build on this foundation.

His measures soon made him short of money. (The warehouses were bulging with coffee, but the naval blockade prevented its sale.) He therefore declared that all land in Java belonged to the sovereign, i.e. the Netherlands, and proceeded to sell land to European planters. Unlike the Company, however, he gave the landowners absolute rights over the people living on the estates. Had his rule continued most of the inhabitants of Java would have become bondsmen.

Daendels also strengthened the defence of Java, including the construction of the first east–west trunk road in Java, completed in one year at a tremendous cost in peasant lives. However, he was recalled in 1811; his successor arrived just in time to surrender Java to the British East India Company.

The decision to invade Java was taken only because the Netherlands was now under French rule; the island itself held no attraction for the East India Company. All that was intended was a punitive expedition. This was planned and mounted by Lord Minto. The orders of the Directors-General of the East India Company were that the Dutch were to be evicted, their installations destroyed, and the island returned to the native rulers. Lord Minto had no intention of obeying. His idea was rather to take over the island as a going concern, using those Dutchmen who were prepared to collaborate.

Raffles

Minto's agent was Thomas Stamford Raffles, later famous as the founder of Singapore. Following the usual practice of those who want to overthrow existing governments, Raffles made approaches to the various rulers who were subject to the Dutch, offering to 'liberate' them from Dutch 'oppression'. The latter pursued the policy now known as 'neutralism', i.e. they put a foot in either camp.

Minto appeared with a fleet of nearly a hundred transports and 12,000 soldiers on 3 August 1811. Six weeks later, the capitulation was signed. Raffles was made Lieutenant Governor-General, and the whole of the Indonesian archipelago came under the control of the East India Company.

Raffles's permanent achievements were in the field of administration. He revised the treaties between the government and the

62

Javanese princes; reorganized the administrative institutions and the judiciary; and reformed the system of taxes and contributions. He tried, but failed, to introduce the jury system into the courts.

Like many new-comers to positions of control, Raffles sought, under cover of some acceptable ideology, to destroy the centres of power in the country. In this he resembled Daendels. Though their approach differed, conditioned by their different national traditions, they both represented the idea that it was now possible to administer a country centrally and with efficiency, instead of leaving power in the hand of local potentates. This was one main achievement, perhaps, of the French Revolution; and in Indonesia both Daendels and Raffles, neither of them Frenchmen, were its disciples.

Under Raffles's rule, Bantam ceased to exist as a sultanate; Cheribon was annexed to Batavia; Jogyakarta was reduced to complete vassalage, and another small state, ruled by the Paku Alam, came into existence. The regents lost the little autonomy Daendels had left them, and became mere officials under direct control of the administrators of the provinces.

Raffles was under instructions to change the system of compulsory deliveries of produce as a means of taxation. The measures he introduced had an additional aim: to destroy the power of the regents. Like Daendels, Raffles declared that all land belonged to the sovereign, that is to his own government. Unlike Daendels, he argued that this was the Oriental theory of the state. He neither took into consideration the fact that the theory had been considerably modified in practice, nor did he justify himself in following it.

Using this concept, he satisfied his need for money by selling cultivated districts to European or Chinese financiers. The peasant, naturally, therefore went into bondage. He also tried to apply the rent system existing in Bengal. It involved making the headman, not the regent, the intermediary between the central government and the cultivator. The first year's collection of taxes were good, and Raffles then decided to do away with the intermediacy of the village head, and to let the land directly to the cultivators.

However, the Directors-General of the East India Company were impressed only by the fact that he failed to balance the budget, and he was recalled in 1815, four years after he took office. Then under an agreement concluded in 1814, Java was handed back to the Netherlands in 1816, and the Dutch government sent out three Commissioners-General to evolve a new system of government. They could have returned to the pre-Raffles order, but decided that there was much merit in his proposals. They retained his system of land-taxes, with the result that the rent received was halved.

Raffles, meanwhile, had been appointed Governor of Benkulen, and in 1819 finally succeeded in planting a trading centre on the island of Singapore, which was then a desolate swamp. He made it a duty-free port, and it quickly flourished as a centre of commerce and shipping. The Dutch had certain claims to the territory, but in a treaty of 1824 they gave them up in exchange for Benkulen. Raffles thus lost his job, returned to England, and died two years later. The city of Singapore is one monument to his memory. The other is his *History of Java*; he was the first Governor of that island to take an intelligent interest in the language, customs, history, and life of the people.

What should perhaps be pointed out is that, for differing reasons, the Dutch East India Company, Daendels, Raffles, and all successive governments of the archipelago have been concerned with the basic problem of economic development, namely how to produce a surplus. It is true, of course, that the foreign governments were concerned with the production of a surplus which would, primarily, benefit the home country, whereas the governments of independent Indonesia, in so far as they have been concerned to produce a surplus, have wished to use it themselves.

It is also true that the form the surplus was to take depended on the interests of the European country. There was really little sense in the Dutch (and much in the British), putting money into the hands of the peasantry, for the Netherlands did not produce manufactured goods, and the demand would have been met by the English manufacturers. Having nothing to offer, the Dutch were compelled to demand taxation in produce which was then shipped to the Netherlands, and only turned into money there.

As it happened, the Dutch system was much better suited to

Javanese conditions than was the English. Raffles's and the Commis-sioners-General attempt to monetize the economy, by making the cultivators pay their rent in cash, placed them in the hands of both the money-lenders and the native chiefs, but failed to increase produc-tion. The Dutch system, while it strengthened the hold of the native chiefs over the cultivators, at least excluded the money-lenders, and did achieve the primary aim of creating a surplus.

Van den Bosch

The Commissioners-General were succeeded by Governor-General Van der Capellen, who is mainly remembered for the Java War of 1825–30, which started during his period of office and as a result of measures he took. The leader of that revolt, Prince Diponegoro, is now regarded as one of the progenitors of Indonesian nationalism, and for that reason alone it is worth considering the war in some detail.

Diponegoro was the elder son of the Sultan of Jogyakarta, and had been expecting to succeed to the throne. But the government at Batavia ruled in favour of his nephew. Diponegoro then declared a 'Holy War' against the 'unbelievers'.

In the principalities, discontent was rife. Daendels and Raffles had so reduced the princely territories that it was difficult for the rulers to provide sufficient land and peasants for their many relatives. To restore their declining incomes, they farmed out villages to Chinese and European entrepreneurs. This raised both the amount extracted from the villages and the income of the princes; it also created resentment among the villagers.

On a tour of inspection through Central Java, Van der Capellen concluded that the entrepreneurs had made illicit use of compulsory labour and ordered the cancellation of their leases. Unfortunately, he also decreed that the leaseholders were to be indemnified by the owners of the land. These, of course, were the princes at Jogyakarta, who naturally thought that Van der Capellen's measures were directed against them, not the entrepreneurs. Not the first time, perhaps, that good intentions have had evil consequences. The aris-tocracy were in no position to indemnify the entrepreneurs, as they had already spent the money paid for their leases. The only courses open to them were ruin or revolt. They joined Diponegoro. The Surakarta aristocracy, unaffected by the decree, remained loyal to the Dutch.

Diponegoro took to the hills and waged guerrilla warfare. He was considerably helped by the sympathy of the people, even when they were not in open revolt. In addition, he showed himself a master of guerrilla tactics. As an opposing force, the Dutch initially had only a small army. However, they were gradually strengthened by troops from Surakarta and the loyal regents of Java, from the princes of Madura, and from northern Celebes. Reinforcements were also brought from Europe, as casualties were high (a result of cholera, not battle). Both sides made a point of destroying all crops, so as to deny them to the enemy; the peasantry starved to death in conse-quence. The rebels were finally worn down, and the end came when Diponegoro's nephew and his men went over to the Dutch. Diponegoro then offered to negotiate and was invited to visit Dutch headquarters. There the Dutch treacherously arrested him and sent him into exile in the Celebes. Nearly 15,000 on the Dutch side had lost their lives, among them 8,000 Europeans; some 200,000 Javanese had died, only about a tenth in battle.

Extraordinarily enough, when the war was over the Dutch did not punish their enemies and reward their friends. Though Surakarta had supported the Dutch, and Jogyakarta had rebelled against them, the territories of both were now further truncated, with both princes receiving annual cash subsidies as compensation. The Susuhunan of Surakarta complained, of course, but did nothing more. The treaties of 1830, then signed, remained in force to the end of Dutch rule in Indonesia.

The five years' war had meant great expense to the Dutch; no sooner had it ended than a further calamity struck them, this time in the Netherlands itself. Belgium, then a part of the kingdom, rose in revolt. When its separation ended the war nine years later, the Netherlands was bankrupt both at home and in the Indies.

Understandably, the need for money took precedence over all other aims of policy. The man of the moment appeared in the shape of Johannes Van den Bosch. Van den Bosch had been in the Indies in the days before Daendels, but due to disagreement between them had had to leave. In 1813, when Europe rebelled against French domination, Van den Bosch joined the Netherlands national movement, held high military positions in the new state, and then retired to devote his time to social welfare. Because of his abilities he was sent on a special mission to the West Indies; on his return he was dispatched to the East Indies to reorganize its economy.

From his experience Van den Bosch believed neither that the Javanese peasant, if set free, would seek his own advantage, nor that he was too lazy to do so. He simply took the view that the people of the island were too ignorant, however willing, to make unaided economic progress. They should be guided by the authorities, taught, and if necessary forced to work. He came to the conclusion that the Javanese peasant's standard of living was higher than that of the Dutch pauper. Hence if the government 'organized' Javanese agriculture to raise its level, it was only doing its duty. Van den Bosch proposed considerably to increase the production of export crops in Java, and to strengthen Dutch commerce and shipping by giving them first option in handling the crop. The result would be, he foresaw, to balance the budget both in Europe and in the Indies.

The system Van den Bosch evolved came to be known as the *Cultuurstelsel*, most descriptively translated, perhaps, as the Forced Cultivation System. The government demanded either payment of the land rent (normally two-fifths of the crop) or the cultivation, in a fifth part of the rice-fields, of a crop indicated by the Director of Cultivation. In other words, the villagers were now saddled with a new tax in the form of compulsory labour. For the cultivation of the crop the labour exacted was not to exceed the amount necessary for producing rice on the same acreage. If the crop exceeded in value the amount of land rent due before the introduction of the system, the surplus would be paid to the villagers. Instead of working on government fields, villagers could be put to work in the factories where the crops, such as sugar and indigo, were prepared for export. These factories were organized and managed by Europeans and Chinese to whom money was advanced by the government, and who received a fixed sum for their services. The villagers were to be paid for all work in the factories or in transporting the products. Formally, all contracts concerning the fields, labour, and transport were freely made between government officials and village head-men; in fact, of course, the village headmen had no option but to accept the terms set by the officials. In brief, the system resulted in the exploitation of Java as though it were a huge government plantation (or labour camp).

Never before had the Dutch intervened so deeply in the economic life of the country. The Company had limited itself to ordering the restriction or extension of production; it had not gone into produc-tion itself; while Daendels and Raffles had thought of 'setting the people free'. But just as the Dutch would never have governed Java without the support of the nobility, so also they were now compelled to turn to them to ensure the success of the Forced Cultivation System. The Java War had brought home to the Dutch how much their position in Java depended on the support of the regents. To ensure the success of the Forced Cultivation System, Van den Bosch abrogated Daendels's and Raffles's reforms, and restored to the regents their former ranks. In addition he guaranteed them hereditary succes-sion in office. This was something they had long desired but never had, and for which there was no sanction in Javanese custom.

The regents were at the peak of the native administration. Below them came a number of district heads, or *wedono*, who were helped by assistant wedono, who had direct supervision over village heads. These, and their subordinates, were drawn from the villagers; the assistant wedono and above came from the noble class.

Alongside the native officials Van den Bosch placed Dutch administrators. It will be remembered that the Company had appointed supervisors over the production of coffee in the Preanger area. These were given the name of 'controllers' by Van den Bosch, and were charged with new functions. Not only were they to oversee the vast new undertakings of government agriculture, but also they were to keep an eye on the administration of the regents and their subordinates. In order to keep themselves abreast of what was hap-pening in native administration, the controllers were expected to attend meetings, which were held at irregular intervals. They were also responsible for the administration of the ethnic groups in the population who were neither European nor Indonesian. These were the Chinese, Indians, and Arabs, collectively termed 'Foreign Asians'. Senior to the controllers and regents were the Residents. These helped by assistant Residents were responsible for a number of regencies.

To the Dutch the Forced Cultivation System seemed a great success. Between 1831 and 1877 the Netherlands treasury received 823 million guilders from the Indies. Some of this amount amortized the colonial debt, but the rest paid the debts of the Netherlands and the expenses of the war with Belgium, as well as the cost of railways and public works. At the time, the annual budget of the Netherlands was not more than 60 million guilders; the Indies contribution averaged 18 million guilders a year.

Not only was the Netherlands treasury replenished, but also Dutch commerce and shipping were promoted. Until 1830, despite protective tariffs, Dutch shipping in the archipelago had not been able to make much headway against its British competitors. Now a new Company, the Netherlands Trading Company, was set up with the specific function of carrying the produce from the Indies to Amsterdam. This very quickly restored Amsterdam as a centre of commerce for Indies merchandise, and created a prosperous middle class. The Netherlands Trading Company in turn promoted the Dutch merchant fleet, which rapidly became the third largest in the world after the British and the French.

Most of the revenue came from the production of coffee. This was grown in the Preanger area of West Java on government land; it was not therefore a part of the system, since it was not produced by the people to meet tax demands. In the case of this crop, Van den Bosch had simply reinstated the monopoly. The costs of producing the other crops were so high, despite the use of compulsory labour, that the government had difficulty in maintaining their cultivation. Under this system the Javanese grew only a third of the amount they could produce by free labour. To encourage better production, the government gave a certain percentage of the returns to the controllers and the regents, but this only encouraged them to squeeze more out of the people; it did not improve agriculture. However, the profits from coffee made up for the losses from other crops.

The system was repealed in 1869; Van den Bosch was Governor-General only from 1830 to 1833, so he cannot be blamed for the development of the system after his departure. But that it became an onerous burden on the Javanese is undeniable; contrary to Van den Bosch's ideas, the government adopted the principle of 'heads I win, tails you lose'. If the crop failed, the people were left responsible for the loss. Whereas the original intention had been that compulsory labour was a means of paying land-taxes, as the system developed both were exacted. Though only 3 or 4 per cent of the arable soil of Java was used for the required crops, their transport was a heavy weight on the whole people. In addition, the villagers often had to walk many miles to the fields where they were to work for the government. And this was not all. The controllers and the regents extorted what they could from the villagers; the Chinese sugar-mill owners exacted as much as they dared; their compatriots who farmed tolls and market taxes added their own burden. In a number of districts of Java, fields were used for export crops at the expense of rice to such an extent that famine resulted. The picture that emerges is of a submissive Javanese population ruthlessly exploited for the benefit of the Netherlands, with Dutch controllers, Javanese regents, and Chinese tax-farmers adding their further extortions. By making the regents partners in the exploitation of their own people, the Dutch had ensured that the Javanese would be deprived of their natural leaders in any revolt to which they might be driven.

The sudden wealth created by the Indies for the Dutch did not breed generosity among them, but quite the reverse. The more they got, the more they wanted. Government expenses in the Indies were pared to the bone, and educational and social needs went unmet. There is no doubt that the system stunted Javanese social and political development; the country would not present the dejected picture it does now if some of the profits of the Forced Cultivation System had been ploughed back into the country *at the time*. In the meanwhile, consequent on the peaceful conditions reigning after the

Java War, the population increased rapidly, as did the area of land under cultivation. Imports of foreign goods also increased, probably indicating a decline of Javanese handicrafts.

Java derived very few benefits indeed from the system. They were principally in the introduction of new plants; the most important of which were tea, first from China, then from Assam; tobacco; cinnamon; cassava; palm-oil; and cinchona (for quinine).

However, the success of the system in creating a prosperous Dutch trading middle class built up resistance to its own continuance. They demanded that private enterprise be allowed to share in the profits being made. This was the only political division with regard to Java: the Conservatives wished to exploit it as a government preserve, the Liberals wanted private enterprise to have a hand. The latter were helped by the success of *Max Havelaar*, a novel by Douwes Dekker under the pseudonym 'Multatuli' (he who has suffered much). It became a classic of Dutch nineteenth-century literature, and was a criticism not only of the colonial administration and the extortionate regents, but also of those in the Netherlands who were benefiting from the exploitation of Java. The book provided ammunition for those Liberals who wished to change the system of colonial administration for one more in keeping with their own ideas.[2]

In 1848 a Liberal constitution was promulgated in the Netherlands, but it was only some fifteen years later that all forced cultivation was abolished with the exception of sugar and coffee, which alone were profitable. All monopolies also were terminated, and so, after long centuries, the oppression of the Moluccas finally ended. Then, in 1864, an Accountability Act brought the administration of the Netherlands Indies, which had been under the exclusive authority of the king, within the control of the Dutch Parliament. In 1870 all government enterprises in sugar cultivation were abolished. Of the whole Forced Cultivation System only compulsory production of coffee was left, and this dragged on until the end of 1916, when it came to an end in the Preanger area, where it had begun two centuries earlier; a great tribute to its profitability.

The basis for private development in Indonesia was laid by the Agrarian law of 1870, which permitted private individuals and companies to hold an hereditary lease on government domains for seventy-five years. It also allowed them to arrange with the individual owners of the village rice-fields for a lease extending not more than twenty years, or in certain cases not more than five years. Happily, the Law recognized the special character of Indonesian property rights and their variations throughout the archipelago, prohibited the selling of landed property, owned or used by Indonesians, to non-Indonesians, and claimed as government domain those lands to which no Indonesian held a claim.

Thus, the Forced Cultivation System came to an end, and the new period of private enterprise began. The Liberals believed that the loss of revenue from government agriculture would be made up from customs duties and taxes, and expected that the Indies would not only meet its own needs, but also increase its remittances to the Netherlands. They were optimists.

6   Prosperity and Welfare

Growth and Expansion

LIBERAL POLICY IN THE INDIES was initiated in 1870; the
Suez Canal had been opened the previous year. It reduced the cost
of transport, increasing yet further the advantage of steam over sail,
and so widened the market for Indonesian produce. In addition, the
period towards the end of the nineteenth century until the beginning
of the twentieth was one of great economic activity in the world. In
consequence, the country experienced prosperity very quickly,
which the Liberals attributed to free enterprise. The facts do not
quite support this analysis.

It is true that between 1870 and 1885 export crops developed in
astonishing fashion. Sugar more than doubled; tobacco grew tenfold
between 1870 and 1890; tin rose nearly five times between 1870 and
1900. However, coffee, which was still cultivated by the government, also increased. Clearly it was not Liberal principles of production, but an increase in world demand, that was responsible.

The Canal also created a closer link between Europe and the
Indies. If before 1870 the Indies were looked upon as a place of
exile, where went only those who could not make good at home,
with the improved sea communications Dutchmen turned to look
upon their Far Eastern possession as a worthwhile place in which to
work and to take their women. With the Dutchmen came Dutch
capital; there is perhaps no need to underline how in more recent
years the withdrawal of Europeans from Asia has also meant the
departure of private funds.

A number of trading companies and banks were established between 1860 and 1880 with the purpose of financing private agri-cultural enterprises. The most important credit institution, however, was the Netherlands Trading Company which, as we have seen above, had been established at the inception of the Forced Cultiva-tion System. With the termination of that system, it lost its function as the agent for the sale of government products, and turned to finance private promoters; before long it had established itself as a normal bank with branch offices all over the Far East.

It is in this period, too, between 1887 and 1907, that the now giant international oil company, Royal-Dutch Shell, was established. A small oil company was founded in 1890, and immediately began to develop markets throughout the Far East. After a victorious tussle with Standard Oil, it organized all the oil companies of Indonesia into one concern, the Royal Dutch Oil Company. It then combined with the British-owned Shell Transport and Trading Company. In 1907 it organized the production of Indonesian oil under three subsi-diary companies. The yearly output of oil had risen from 300 metric tons in 1889 to 363,000 tons in 1900. The government now inter-vened, and as the result of a Mining Law in 1899 decreed that certain oil-fields were to be reserved for government exploitation. All this was in the days when oil was used principally for lighting; after the internal-combustion engine was developed, the oil-fields of Sumatra were to acquire strategic significance.

The Liberals had argued that the general prosperity in the Indies which would follow on the adoption of their system would provide enough revenue to compensate for the loss of profits from government cultivation. At the end of the century most of government revenue came from taxation, and only a small amount from cultivation (principally coffee). However, the government was in constant deficit, mainly because its taxation system was inadequate for the task of siphoning off enough for public expenditure. Three-quarters of taxa-tion was collected from Indonesians, who were the poorest section of the community. There had been an increasing influx of Europeans in private employment in the last quarter of the nineteenth century and they rapidly came to outnumber the government officials. In addition, a class of wealthy planters had come into being. It was this group which, in relation to its income, was insufficiently taxed. But this was not surprising, as direct taxes on income were not levied in the Netherlands itself until 1913; they appeared in the Indies five years earlier. In consequence, government deficits in the last quarter of the nineteenth century had to be covered by loans.

The deficits themselves were a consequence of Liberal policy. The entrepreneurs demanded good communications and security if their enterprises were to flourish; these cost money. For less interested reasons the Liberals also demanded extension of education, for both Europeans and Indonesians, and better local government. They also demanded pacification of the islands other than Java.

For the last quarter of the century the Netherlands government, conforming with the contemporary prevalent fashion of imperialism, pressed its claims to the islands surrounding Java, which previously it had largely neglected. Here as ever the fear was that if Batavia did not assert its rights first, some other European power, or the United States, would step in. Batavia had received a warning in the middle of the century, when James Brooke made himself Rajah of Sarawak and acquired Labuan for the British Crown, becoming its first Governor. The Dutch protested, but were unable to do more, as the treaty of 1824 had limited Dutch rights to the area south of the Straits of Malacca. The same treaty prevented it occupying Atjeh. The temptation, even the need, to do so went on increasing. The Atjeh-nese chiefs attacked any shipping that came within reach of their ports, English, Dutch, American, and Italian, and attempted to obtain outside support, turning first to Turkey, who however was both unwilling and unable to help them. At the same time, the obligation to curb piracy in these seas lay exclusively with the Dutch.

Then in 1871 the Dutch concluded a treaty with Britain whereby the British gained the Dutch Gold Coast, and withdrew their objections to a possible occupation of Atjeh by the Dutch. Even so, the cost of a war with Atjeh was a deterrent to the government at Batavia. However, the Atjehnese went on marauding and now sought support from the United States and Italy. These approaches were not even entertained, but they served to accentuate Batavia's fears that if it did not extend its control over Atjeh, another power would. Emissaries from Batavia were sent to Atjeh to secure an agreement that would satisfy both parties by guaranteeing the safety of shipping in Atjehnese waters. They were unable to obtain satisfaction and declared hostilities. Though the first expeditionary force landed in 1873, the war proved to be a long-drawn-out and expensive affair, which ended only in 1908. Even then, the means by which it was terminated sowed seeds of further trouble, though not for the Dutch. The Adviser to the Netherlands Indies government on Islamic Affairs, a well-known scholar by the name of Snouck Hurgronje, counselled that the war could be ended by befriending the traditional leaders, who were opposed to the religious dignitaries. The policy worked, but in 1941, when the Dutch administration collapsed in face of the Japanese invasion, the religious leaders had their revenge. They sided with the invaders and slaughtered the hereditary chiefs.

Batavia consolidated its rule elsewhere also. In 1894 the island of Lombok was brought under direct Dutch rule. At the beginning of the twentieth century the Sultanates on the southwestern peninsula of Celebes were occupied by Dutch troops. The potentates of the other territories not under direct Dutch rule, some 250 in all, of widely different sizes, were made to sign a formula which empowered the government to direct them how to rule. This involved the *de facto* transfer of all authority to Dutch officials.

By 1910 the job was done, and the boundaries of present-day Indonesia had been drawn. It is well to remember how recently most of the territories of the Indies have been exposed to Western administration, which when it came was not intensive. It is Java, pre-eminently, which has been truly colonized for a long period of time. This goes some way to explain the very different attitudes of the Javanese compared with the other peoples of the archipelago.

This act of expansion was political in motivation; it was not dictated by the needs of private enterprise, which largely remained limited to Java and Sumatra. Needless to say, the expansionists got little thanks for their pains. The Europeans accused them of 'capitalist imperialism', and those they pacified resented the fact that they could no longer prey on their neighbours. But if large units are now the order of the day, there can be no doubt that Governor-Generals Van Wijck and Van Heutsz, who drew the final boundaries of the Indies, did well to ensure that as many peoples as possible were brought under one government. The Indonesians owe their importance in Southeast Asia primarily to these two men.

Welfare

While the task of unifying the archipelago was in its final stages, the government embarked on a new policy of welfare, which has been called the 'Ethical Policy'. It sprang from the notion that since the Netherlands had drawn so much out of the Indies at the time of the Forced Cultivation System, it was in honour bound to help the people of the archipelago in their need for welfare. In 1901 the government declared that one of the principles on which it would base its future policy would be the 'moral duty of the Netherlands towards the people of the Indies'. However, it was only seven years later that the finances of the Netherlands and the Indies were definitely separated, which had the effect of preventing any transfer of a surplus from Batavia to The Hague. This was just as well, as the first decade of the century saw another boom period for the Indies, after near-bankruptcy in 1899. Cane-sugar, which had been depressed as a result of competition with beet-sugar, recovered after an agreement reached at a conference in Brussels, and entered upon its period of greatest prosperity. The production of tea increased five times, while rubber rose from scratch to 15,000 tons. Investment funds flowed in from Europe. Oil production rose from 363,000 tons in 1900 to 1,540,000 tons in 1914. Not only Royal-Dutch Shell but also Standard Oil were now working oil-fields in Sumatra. It was at this time, too, that export production began to move away from Java to the other islands, principally Sumatra. Consequently, state revenue rose, most of it from taxes, and only a quarter from govern-ment enterprises. This permitted the authorities to devote more funds to Indonesian welfare.

And here we must draw attention to the sad fact that from the beginning of this century, as far as the experts can judge, Javanese welfare has been generally diminishing. No changes of policy or government have succeeded in arresting the decline. The chief reason for it is the great increase of population in Java. This had risen from some $2\frac{1}{2}$ million people in 1800 to 28 millions in 1900 (it continued to increase to 63 millions in 1961). The government conceived it as its duty to increase the arable land available, and did so by vast and expensive irrigation works. But the population more than caught up with the augmented acreage. Attempts were made to encourage migration to the less populated islands; but these are less fertile than Java, and the numbers who migrated were more than replaced by natural increase.

A peasant economy is typically one where money is very scarce. Hence the peasant is only too prone to mortgage his future by placing himself in debt to the money-lender. The Agrarian Law of 1870, happily, had forbidden the alienation of land by foreclosure, and so had prevented catastrophes such as occurred in Burma, where during the depression of the nineteen-thirties it was found that Indian money-lenders owned most of the rice land of the Irrawaddy delta. Nevertheless, as long as credit was not forthcoming the Javanese peasant continued to fall into debt. The government therefore organ-ized a number of rural credit institutions. In 1917 there were over 1,000, which extended credit to 1,300,000 peasants. Village banks were also established, numbering 2,000 in 1917, with over 600,000 depositors.

The increase of population in Java was undoubtedly due to the fact that, to serve its economic interests, the government gave more attention to that island than to any other, and ensured that absolute peace reigned. The growth of population was further accelerated by the introduction of hygienic measures. Bubonic plague appeared in 1905; it was stamped out in a struggle lasting twenty-five years. Work on beri-beri, long a scourge in the archipelago, opened the chapter on vitamins in medical science.

But though the government was concerned to maintain and if possible improve the material welfare of the Javanese, it wanted to do so only in a traditional context. It did not envisage that the Indonesians would change their culture. It can be argued that the only hope for Indonesia is that the agrarian base of her economy be changed to an industrial. Whatever may be the case, the Dutch, both as a government and as a people, were most averse to exposing Indonesians to Western influences. Among these was education.

No schools for Indonesians existed before 1854. Two teachers' colleges were opened in 1866 and 1867. It was the realization among enlightened Dutchmen of the need for schools in Indonesia that first gave rise to the pressure for the 'Ethical Policy'. One of the greatest stumbling-blocks to the spread of education was the insistence by Dutch educational experts that the schools should be comparable to those in the Netherlands. To have instituted such schools all over Java would have taken up most of the state's revenue. It was only when the decision was taken to set up 'village' schools that education began to make headway. The government gave funds for school buildings and provided the wood from which the villagers could make furniture for their school. It helped to find teachers, usually those who had completed elementary instruction in a 'second-class' school (to distinguish it from the Dutch schools), and paid their salaries. Apart from this the school was maintained by village funds, with each child paying a mite. Needless to say, to provide the institution was not enough; there was much resistance to overcome. In the first place, the peasant parents saw little use in a school which took their children away from work in the fields. Then sheer novelty was a factor against acceptance. Lastly, it was an institution intro-duced by an alien government, and consequently suspect.

Education therefore developed slowly. In 1903 there were 190,000 pupils in the Indies; in 1913 227,000; in 1923 700,000; and in 1940 2 millions. Set against the numbers in the population, these figures were not spectacular; in addition, however, the education provided was largely limited to primary and secondary. There was almost no way in which an Indonesian could prepare himself in an Indonesian school for the senior positions in the state and the higher professions; he had to move to the alien environment of a Dutch school and so prepare himself for a university in the Netherlands.

It is also true, unfortunately, that there was little room for the Western-educated in the Indies economy. It was, as we have implied, a plantation economy, in which the supervisors were European, the subordinates Indonesian. The Europeans were concerned with, broadly speaking, the technical and commercial aspects of production; the Indonesians remained simple cultivators. Thus the division between Western and Indonesian spheres of activity remained sharp; it was made sharper still towards the end of the nineteenth century. Because of the slumps in economic activity, the individual planters were driven out of business, and their estates taken over by financial firms based in the Netherlands, who appointed managers to control the estates. This meant, of course, that control of production now left the Indies. Imports and exports were concentrated in the hands of a few Dutch firms; while the intermediary trading functions between these firms and the Indonesian consumer and producer were performed by Chinese. Of the modern sectors of social life, it was the civil service alone that was open to Indonesians, and then only if they were of the nobility. With increased administrative responsibilities, it became necessary to train the corps on modern lines. In Indonesia as elsewhere, this introduced Western education into the country, as the Dutch set up the appropriate schools, initially reserved for the nobility. Some difficulty was at first found in convincing parents of the merit of this innovation, but by the end of the century there were over 80,000 pupils, many in mission schools.

31 Indonesia has long been a peasant economy and in the years which followed 1799 and the end of the Company, peasants were exploited by their European rulers. A characteristic bullock cart in present-day Central Java on its way to market.

32 Thomas Stamford Raffles (1781–1826), Lieutenant Governor-General of Java for the British East India Company from 1811 to 1816, reorganized the administration.

33 (*right*) Raffles' ground was prepared by Herman Willem Daendels (1762–1818), his predecessor as Governor-General.

34 (*far right*) The progenitor of nationalism in Indonesia was Prince Diponegoro (1785–1855) who led a revolt known as the Java War (1825–30) against the Dutch.

35 A nineteenth-century drawing of a Javanese in war-dress.

36 (*left*) Much of the Dutch strength depended on the local rulers. This early photograph shows the Susu-hanan (or emperor) of Surakarta together with the Dutch Resident.

37 Johannes Van den Bosch (1780–1844) was appointed Governor-General in 1830. He introduced the *Cultuurstelsel* or Forced Cultivation System which improved productivity though without benefiting the peasantry.

38, 39, 40 The products of the ensuing agricultural boom created by the Forced Cultivation System were tea (*above*), sugar-cane (*left*), and tobacco (*below*) which have remained important items in the economy.

41 The Dutch empire in the Indies was bounded by the British. A nineteenth-century engraving illustrates the hoisting of the Union Jack at Port Moresby in Southeast New Guinea which became a British Protectorate in 1885.

42 (*right above*) The Dutch acquired Atjeh in Sumatra at the expense of a war which lasted 35 years. 1894: the Universal Dutch Staff in the *Kraton* (palace) of the Sultan of Kota Radja. 43 (*centre*) 1901: Dutch troops victorious after a sanguinary battle in the district of Malaboe. 44 (*below*) 1901: General van Heutsz with his staff at Baté Ilië.

45 In 1941 Indonesians were still predominantly in menial occupations. A Dutch planter is driven round his sugar estate.

46 Between 1800 and 1900 the population of Java had increased by 25½ million. Forest land in Sumatra had to be cleared to absorb some of the surplus.

47 The international oil company, Royal Dutch, was established in 1890. It eventually combined with the British-owned Shell Transport and Trading Company.

7   Growth of Nationalism

Westernization

BECAUSE ONLY A VERY FEW INDONESIANS were given
Western education, lop-sided social development for Indonesia
followed. For whilst on the one hand the Indies were increasingly
entering the world, the peasantry were not acquiring the knowledge
which would have enabled them to understand it. Only the few
educated Indonesians were in this position. In consequence, the
various societies which composed the Indies suffered a radical
change. Before the coming of the West, the prince and the peasant
participated in the same culture; it permitted the peasant to understand, and therefore in some measure to check, his prince's actions.
Under the new dispensation, the peasants were blind, and only the
favoured few could see. Naturally enough, in crises the unseeing
peasants followed the few with sight.

This situation was to assume greater importance as time wore on,
for increasingly the peasant's world became out of joint. We have
mentioned that the 'Ethical Policy' consisted of attempts to improve
the standard of living of the Javanese peasant. But they were all
defeated by the continuing population increase. To repeat, however,
these attempts were made in a traditional context; there was, for
example, no serious attempt to industrialize the country. For neither
in Japan nor in the Netherlands itself has rapid population growth
on a restricted area inhibited economic development. The reasons
that it did so in Java must be sought in sociological, not purely in
economic or demographic terms. More basic, perhaps, was that all

efforts to ameliorate the peasant's lot were those of outsiders to the society, that is to say the Dutch. However well intentioned, they were not in the position of having to feel the impact of change themselves. The peasant, for his part, knew that he would not be permitted to step outside his accustomed path, and that in any case the government had taken it upon itself to look after him. In consequence, there emerged no solution, from within Javanese society, to the problem of economic stagnation.

The 'Ethical Policy' inaugurated at the turn of the century lasted until its abandonment in the great slump of 1930. During this period the standard of living seems to have risen until 1913, declined to 1925, risen again for three years, and fallen suddenly in 1930. Though the Indonesian was probably better off in 1930 than he had been in 1900, what he would remember would not be the rise from 1900 to 1913, but the fall afterwards. And those who suffered most were the educated and politically the most articulate classes.

Paradoxically, despite these variations in the standard of living of the Javanese peasant, the Indies economy continued to develop at a steady rate. Exports, which had been worth 16 million guilders in 1825, rose to 230 million in 1900 and 2,225 million in 1920, representing a cumulative rate of growth of some $5\frac{1}{2}$ per cent per annum. (A fully developed economy which grows at this rate is an object of admiration.) Imports, equally, had been worth only 12·5 million guilders in 1825; they were worth 176 million guilders in 1900 and 1,126 million in 1920, a cumulative rate of increase of some 5 per cent. But it was the Europeans and the Chinese who became richer; the Indonesians simply became more numerous.

It would be a mistake, however, to place too much emphasis on economic factors in the genesis of nationalism. The economic discontents of the time may have provided fuel for the fire, but it was lit much more by the feeling, among the few educated Indonesians, that they were not being given their rightful place in the sun. This emerges very clearly from the letters of *Raden Adjeng*[3] Kartini, with whom the modern Indonesian nationalist movement may be considered to have started. Kartini was the daughter of a regent, one of the traditional nobility who, as we have seen, were the underpinning of Dutch rule in the Indies. In brief, she felt that the Dutch having introduced Indonesians to Western civilization, now attempted to limit their access to it. This was to have unfortunate consequences for the rulers.

A feeling of injustice, however, is not enough to start a nationalist movement. Organization is just as, if indeed not more, important. This was facilitated by the measures the Dutch themselves took at the beginning of the century.

The Indies were then closely controlled from The Hague. The local organ of government was the Governor-General, with a Council composed of a few high officials. The Indonesians were under their own 'appointed or recognized heads'; in particular, the villages were guaranteed the right of electing their own headmen and managing their own affairs.

This system was incompatible with the development of private enterprise. Accordingly, in 1903 a Decentralization Law was passed. It prescribed the election of Europeans to local councils, and further declared that meetings in this connexion would be permitted (previously, no political gatherings had been allowed). This soon became recognized as a right, and was confirmed by law in 1919. Similarly, the shackles were taken off the press. At the turn of the century it consisted mostly of European papers or Indonesian papers owned by Europeans. They were all, however, subject to censorship. A new press regulation in 1906 substituted punitive for preventive supervision.

In addition, the number of debating chambers proliferated. Between 1905 and 1908 several local government councils were formed. Each council comprised Europeans and Indonesians, as well as Chinese where they had important interests. Though the people were represented in these councils, they did not govern. The duty of the councillors was to represent the interests of their locality, but decisions were taken by the civil service.

Indonesians were now able to disseminate their opinions through both the press and voluntary assemblies; the growth of political movements followed naturally. In 1908 the Budi Utomo (High Endeavour) was founded. Its members largely came from the

Javanese aristocracy. Like Kartini it advocated the development of traditional and Western education among Indonesians (it chose Malay, or Javanese, as its medium) and the advancement of agriculture, industry, and commerce. A year after its foundation, Budi Utomo had 10,000 members, including aristocrats, intellectuals, and officials.

Students from the Indies had been slowly accumulating in the Netherlands. By 1908 they, both Indonesians and Eurasians, numbered twenty-three, and formed the Indies Society, which was to play a leading role in the nationalist movement.

The students in Holland were important in that they were an élite; but there were other educated Indonesians also. After the turn of the century the demand for Western education was always far greater than the supply of opportunities for the successful graduates. It is not difficult to see why. Not only did government service carry prestige, but also there were few other employment opportunities, while European incomes, which required Western education, were very much greater than Indonesian. (It was only later that Indonesians came to realize that Western birth or at least Western paternal descent was a criterion as important as education.) In 1929, 69 per cent of Europeans in Java had incomes of over 2,100 guilders a year. In contrast, over 80 per cent of Indonesians in Java had an annual income of less than 300 guilders.

The thirst for the West had found secular expression in Budi Utomo; it took religious form with the founding of the Muhammadiyah in 1912. This association sought to harmonize Western knowledge with the basic teachings of Islam, and for this purpose took its inspiration direct from the two holy books, the Koran and the Hadith, or Tradition, ignoring the interpretations which had accumulated over the centuries.

Both Budi Utomo and the Muhammadiyah were intellectual in type; understandably, they had little influence on the mass of the people. This deficiency was to be remedied by a new organization, which sprang from middle-rank Javanese traders who organized the Sarekat Islam (Muslim Society) on a nation-wide basis in 1912.

The leaders of the new association emphasized that they intended to maintain unwavering loyalty to the government. Their principal aims were the improvement of commercial organization among Indonesians, and the support of Islam. But Islam meant more to the ordinary person in Indonesia than did either Western lore or commercial enterprise; and it was the banner under which he expressed his discontent with Dutch rule, made more specific by the economic decline which began about 1913. By 1917 the Sarekat Islam had 800,000 members; it was the first mass political organization in Indonesia.

Up to this point, however, it would be difficult to maintain that these movements were nationalist, in the sense that they believed in the unity of the people of the Indies. Their efforts were rather devoted to Westernization. But change was at hand.

Nationalism

Despite European resistance, a Law School was opened in 1909. In 1913, however, when it was proposed to open a new Medical School, the European Medical Association protested. This was strongly resented by, among others, one of the founders of Budi Utomo, Dr Tjipto, a Javanese who had been awarded a Dutch order of distinction for abandoning a lucrative practice to do plague work under the government. He joined a Eurasian and another Indonesian in founding a new political association, the National Indies Party.

Based on Eurasian-Indonesian co-operation, with the motto 'The Indies for those who make their home there', the National Indies Party had about 6,000 Eurasian and 1,300 Indonesian members, and was somewhat Marxist in outlook. It expressed the resentment felt by Eurasians against the increasing numbers of Europeans who came out to the Indies with the intention of retiring to Holland as soon as they had achieved financial success. The Indies government suppressed it within a year.

Despite its brief life, the National Indies Party strongly affected Indonesian nationalism. From the party the Sarekat Islam borrowed the idea of a nation when it called its first National Congress in 1916. As yet, however, this did not mean independence; it only wanted 'to raise native society to nation', but under the Netherlands flag and with government support.

It was not only through the National Indies Party that the European community affected Indonesian nationalism. In 1914 a recent Dutch arrival founded the Indies Social Democratic Association. It became increasingly radical, and absorbed the Marxist-inclined members of the National Indies Party after the latter's suppression. In order to capture the mass base necessary for the revolution at which it aimed, some of the Indonesian leaders of Sarekat Islam were induced to join the Association, and thus its ideas were spread among their own members.

In 1916 certain powers were transferred from the Netherlands to the Indies, and a Volksraad (People's Council) was set up. The Council had no legislative power, but the government had to consult it in certain matters of finance, including the budget, and also before imposing military duty, and might take its advice on other matters. Though half of the members, mostly Indonesians, were elected, the electorate consisted of members of the local councils; most of them were officials; and about two-thirds were nominated, so that the People's Councillors were indirectly government nominees. (It should, however, be noted that officials in the Netherlands Indies were given very great freedom to criticize government policy.)

Legislative changes simultaneously provided for greater Indonesian representation. From 1917 Indonesians were elected to the local councils; and from about that time, also, the practice of ensuring a European majority was abandoned.

If anything, these measures encouraged the extremists. Marxist infiltration of the Sarekat Islam bore fruit at its 1917 Congress. It was not opposed to evil, that is to any foreign, capitalism; the Sarekat Islam's funds were largely provided by Indonesian capitalists (the same distinction, for much the same reasons, was later made in sovereign Indonesia). It now called for independence, whether obtained peacefully or otherwise.

In setting up the Council, the Governor-General of the day showed his sympathy for Indonesian aspirations by nominating as members Socialists and left-wing Nationalists, including the leader of the

Sarekat Islam. He also opened the People's Council in May 1918 with a speech foreshadowing the autonomy of the Indies to a much greater extent than the Act instituting the Council had permitted.

In answer, the Council's first session rejected a proposal that a loyal cable be addressed to the Queen of the Netherlands, and compelled the government to permit debates in Malay, though for most of the members this was as foreign as Dutch. (This was perhaps poetic justice, for the Dutch community had discouraged Indonesians from speaking Dutch to them.)

At the second session of the People's Council, towards the end of 1918, the criticisms of the government became more violent than ever. At the same time the Governor-General heard of a revolutionary outbreak in the Netherlands. He thereupon announced that he would alter the relations of government and Council. Even more extreme demands were then made, which were only quelled by the Governor-General's appointment of a Revisional Commission.

Flushed with success, the Sarekat Islam at its Congress that year put forward demands for wide social reforms, and indicated that if the government did not undertake them, the Sarekat Islam would. This policy drew in more members, and at its fourth Congress in 1919 there were $2\frac{1}{2}$ million represented. When the Congress refused to adopt extreme measures, the revolutionary section formed itself into the Partai Komunis di India (PKI), or Communist Party of the Indies. It is worth noting that of its principal officers, two were Javanese and two Dutch.

In 1920 the membership of the People's Council was raised to forty-nine, of whom at least half were to be Indonesians. Twenty-four were to be elected, at least half of them Indonesians, and twenty-four, including eight Indonesians, were to be nominated. Two-thirds of the electors, however, were still nominated.

Furthermore, the revised Fundamental Law of the Netherlands of 1922 ruled that all powers other than those specially reserved were to be considered delegated to the government of the Indies, the reverse of the previous position. This now involved drafting a new constitution for the Indies.

In the background the training of Indonesian students, both in Holland and in Indonesia, to European levels continued. One might have expected that they would take over jobs in accordance with their qualifications. Unfortunately, European vested interests proved too strong. It was decreed that the senior administrative positions, that is those in the European Civil Service, should be filled only by Europeans (including Eurasians), and Indonesians would be restricted to the Indonesian Civil Service. In the newer corps, the specialist services, Indonesians were to be admitted on the same basis as Europeans. But though this was the higher-paid service, it did not include, nor with rare exceptions lead to, the senior administrative positions.

The significance of this decision needs to be emphasized. Before Indonesians had been trained on Western lines, their restriction to the indigenous administration was unavoidable, and need not necessarily have implied racial discrimination. Once they had acquired Western knowledge, however, the same limitation meant that it was no longer their training, but their 'race', that mattered.

It is to be noted, also, that the definition of race was legal. The ethnic groups of Indonesia differ widely among themselves; but these distinctions came to have little significance compared with those between the legally defined groups of Dutch, Indonesians, and 'Foreign Orientals', i.e. Chinese and Arabs. With a unitary salary scale instituted in the specialist services, the only field where Indo-nesians could compete against Eurasians, the latter increasingly cast off their identification with Indonesians, which had expressed itself in the National Indies Party, and began to form close links with the Europeans.

The consequences of this new departure were not slow in emerg-ing. A number of political parties founded in 1916 and 1917 and based on the principle of association did not survive the division into 'races'. In the Netherlands, the Indies Society became purely Indo-nesian in 1922 and excluded Eurasians. It now called itself the Perhimpunan Indonesia (Indonesian Union). A year later it declared itself for the independence of Indonesia, to be attained by the unity of all Indonesian groups and classes on the basis of non-co-operation with the Dutch. Generally, its members had a Marxist orientation, and some emerged as members of the Communist Party.

The depression which followed the First World War produced a number of communist-inspired strikes. The government embarked on a policy of repression which resulted in economic discontent and encouraged extreme views. The radicals in the Sarekat Islam, considering the moment propitious, tried at the 1923 Congress to bring the whole organization under communist control. Though they failed in their main purpose, they succeeded in drawing away many of its members to a new organization, the Red Sarekat Islam, which adapted communist policy to rural requirements.

In the meantime, the new constitution for the Indies had been going through the Dutch Parliament. Contrary to the Fundamental Law, the Indies was not given independence as an integral part of the commonwealth. More important, perhaps, was that whereas previously there had been a single electorate for the People's Council, now each of the three population groups was to elect its representatives separately. This was an attempt to ensure that the interests of the Dutch community would not be superseded by those of the majority.

Had the single electorate remained, it is probable that an increasing proportion of those elected to the People's Council would have been Indonesian. Whether, in consequence, they would have paid regard only to Indonesian interests is an open question. It is at least possible that the lines of conflict would have been drawn on economic rather than 'racial' lines. The division of the electorate by 'race' however, ensured that those elected would pay virtually exclusive regard to their own ethnic group.

By restricting the powers of the People's Council, and by ensuring that the Indonesians would never have an effective majority there, the Dutch guaranteed irresponsible criticism of the government. Since the Indonesians could not expect to govern, there was nothing to moderate their acerbity.

In the twenties the Perhimpunan Indonesia in Holland began to exert a strong influence on the nationalist movement. Government repression in Indonesia was so effective that the Sarekat Islam was compelled to pursue a moderate policy. The Indonesian graduates who returned from Europe began to take over positions of leadership in the organization, and broadened its interests to include the promotion of education and the study of economic conditions. Schools of various types were founded, all outside the official educational system and therefore known as 'wild'; co-operative organizations were set up; and even the foundation of an Indonesian bank was attempted. One may describe these activities as a withdrawal from Indies society, as then constituted, to a purely Indonesian one. The returned members of the Perhimpunan Indonesia also established a number of 'study clubs' in the main cities between 1923 and 1927. One of these was to give birth to the nationalist movement's strongest leadership.

The post-war slump ended in 1925 and the Indies entered upon a boom which lasted until the great depression of 1929, reaching its peak in 1928. This did not prevent the communists organizing strikes in 1925, and attempting a revolution in 1926. These were all suppressed without difficulty.

As a response to the revolt of 1926, the government was induced to strengthen its repressive apparatus as well as to improve contacts between officials and the people. The Communist Party was thereby effectively broken up, with the result that the Sarekat Islam was left the undisputed leader of nationalism.

In 1926 a new Governor-General took office; he followed a liberal policy towards the right of association. The next year the members of the study club at Bandung formed the Partai Nasional Indonesia (Indonesian National Party), or PNI, as it was usually called. Its chairman, Sukarno, now President of Indonesia, was then a recently graduated engineer (who, however, unlike the other members of the club, had not been out of Indonesia). The PNI picked up many of the remnants of the Communist Party, and within two years had over 10,000 members. With the support of the leaders of the Sarekat Islam it established a federation of all the important nationalist organizations, and moved them into more extreme channels. The party wanted complete economic and political independence for Indonesia, with a government elected by and responsible to the people. Following the lead of the Perhimpunan

Indonesia, it claimed that this goal could be reached only by non-co-operation with the Dutch, through the united efforts of the Indonesian people. Immediately the party, like the Sarekat Islam, began to build up labour organizations, to develop co-operatives and to support the 'wild schools'. Non-co-operation was to remain the inspiration of Indonesian nationalism.

The nationalist leaders were of course recruited from Western-educated Indonesians, of whom there were not many. Initially, as mentioned above, the nobility had been favoured; in 1912–13, for instance, all of the forty Indonesian students in the Law College were from that class. Thereafter, secondary education was opened to talent, provided the parents could pay the fees, which were high for them. Consequently, those who acquired Western education in the Netherlands Indies were relatively few. In 1930–1 there were only 178 Indonesians in institutions of university level, at a time when the population numbered some 59 millions. At the secondary level, both academic and vocational, there were only 6,085 Indonesians being given instruction in Dutch. At the primary levels, the number of Indonesians given Western education amounted to only 83,655.

Few though the educated were, many of them were fated to un-employment; at best, the jobs they got were at levels lower than their training warranted. The reason was to be found in the country's economic structure. The Netherlands Indies was a plantation economy, in which a few Western managers organized the labour of a large number of unskilled Indonesians. The typical enterprise was the sugar estate. There had, of course, been some mechanization. Railways had been introduced towards the end of the nineteenth century; sugar factories had been set up at about the same time. But it was only when the Indies were cut off from Holland, during the First World War, that any decisive steps were taken to industrialize, and they were not great. Textile manufacture, for instance, often the first step in industrialization, did not begin until the nineteen-thirties, and then it consisted only of weaving.

In brief, industrialization of the type which would employ the Western-educated was merely creeping along. Consequently, the only openings for them were in government service. Unfortunately, even in prosperous times these vacancies could not increase by a yearly rate of more than 2 per cent; in contrast, Western education of Indonesians was increasing at nearly 7 per cent per annum.

There were, of course, certain commercial occupations attached to the plantation economy which might have provided employment for those with Western secondary education. But such jobs were virtually all in the hands of the Chinese. For various reasons few Indonesians had or have the determination or ability to compete with them (a well-known exception are the Menangakabau of Central Sumatra).

Thus the main consequence of expanding Western education without increasing the demand for its products was to frustrate Indonesians. Having prepared themselves, as they thought, for Western employment, they found that it was not for them, and that the jobs they could have had were held by Dutchmen and Eurasians.

The observer, looking at this picture, is bound to ask why the Netherlands Indies government did nothing to improve matters. If it was indeed impossible to provide employment for the Western-educated, why were so many produced? Since the Dutch had no intention of training the Indies for independence, the argument that Western education is necessary for an independent state in the modern world would have had no weight. The answer seems to be that once the schools had been launched, they themselves became vested interests, further strengthened by the lack of other employment opportunities. The demand for education was so great that the Western-educated had no difficulty in setting up the 'wild schools' mentioned earlier, distinct from the state system. By 1938 there were over 2,000 such institutions, the most famous among them being the Taman Siswa, which taught self-reliance. Needless to say, they simply added to the pressure of demand for employment which did not exist.

Weaker Links

The year 1929 marked the onset of the world depression. Even more, perhaps, than defeat by the Japanese thirteen years later, it cast doubt on the right of the Dutch to rule the Indies. The Indonesians, whose faith in the justice of the Indies administration was hardly unanimous, now lost their assurance of economic welfare at Dutch hands. Just as important was the fact that the depression considerably weakened the links of the Indies with the Netherlands.

After Britain's departure from the Gold Standard, Japan devalued the yen, with the result that her goods became virtually irresistible. To control imports, measures were taken which had the effect of stimulating local industry. Indonesian weaving was encouraged and grew at a rapid pace, and so did Indonesian, as distinct from estate, rubber production. Nevertheless, it was of course European industry which expanded most quickly. Much of the capital invested in these new concerns, however, was not Dutch, but foreign. As a result of all these measures the Indies came to import more from Asia and to export less to her. This was at the expense of Europe, from whom the Indies now imported less, but to which it exported more. In other words, the Indies decreased its dependence on Europe; within Europe it had decreased its dependence on the Netherlands.

The slump also gave the greatest impetus yet to the introduction of Indonesians into the modern economy. Lower profits in European firms led to the replacement of expatriate European employees by Eurasians or Indonesians. The European population itself rapidly declined, large numbers returning to Europe. The Japanese set up their own chains of shops to sell their goods, instead of using the Chinese as distributors, and recruited Indonesians.

But whilst openings were created for Indonesians in business, they were closed in the clerical occupations. With the fall of exports and of production generally, government revenues fell, and a policy of retrenchment was adopted. Salaries were cut; a stop was put to recruitment of officials; and many were pensioned off. This naturally increased the discontent among the intelligentsia.

If the slump forced economic self-sufficiency on the Indies, the European community had already, over a period of years, reached a social self-sufficiency. Many Europeans were in the labouring class, or served as shop-assistants. In consequence, whereas in 1900 the European community was detached from native life but had no complete independent life, by 1930 it lived within its own world, with its own cultural interests and with trade unions and labour politics, alongside, but wholly separate from the native world. Political activity in the community, naturally enough, took on all the hues present in the Netherlands.

Such social independence required large numbers. In 1930 of the population there was 1 European to every 244 Indonesians. Further, more, the European community was becoming native to the Indies. In 1930 nearly 70 per cent of the Europeans in the Indies were born there. Also, the number of European women born outside the Indies more than doubled between 1900 and 1930. Inevitably, their presence exerted a pressure against mixing with the 'natives'.

Those who were born in the Indies still, in 1930, predominated in government service, sugar plantations, and other occupations where they lived inland and had dealings with the people; the foreign-born, however, who knew the people least, predominated in towns and occupations where they hardly saw the people save in a menial guise. Even in the government service, there was a great increase of specialists, appointed because of their expertise, not their knowledge of the country. In brief, the rift between Europeans and Indonesians had become both socially and economically much wider.

Furthermore, the European community as a whole in 1930 was less Dutch and more 'Foreign European' than it had been in 1900. Whereas the Dutch had a long tradition of mixing with the people of the country, as indeed was their duty, the other Europeans were there simply because of the opportunities offered.

The Dutch community's response to the growth of Indonesian nationalism took the form of a powerful conservative association, the Vaderlandsche Club, founded in 1929, whose aim was to maintain the link with the Netherlands and the predominance of Dutch authority and the Dutch ruling group throughout the Indies. They obtained one of their objectives at the end of the year. Sukarno and other leaders of his organization were arrested; he was sentenced to imprisonment for three years (of which he served two). The only opposition to the Club consisted of a number of intellectuals. They formed a political and cultural movement to work for an Indies Commonwealth united with the Netherlands. It published a periodical called De Stuw (Forward Movement), and was called after it.

Though some of their members were to achieve prominence later, the group had little support from the community.

Two years after the foundation of the Club, in 1931, a Governor-General was appointed who gave the political police their head. Indonesian nationalists were persecuted, Dutch liberals in the Indies were kept under supervision; the police tried to keep the Dutch community in ignorance of home opinion and home opinion unaware of repression in the Indies.

It did not take long for the nationalists to fall foul of the police. Sukarno was released on the last day of 1931, and two prominent members of the Perhimpunan Indonesia in Holland returned to Indonesia in 1932. They were Mohammad Hatta, who had been its leader, and *Sutan*[4] Sjahrir, then a law student. Both came from Sumatra, and found it difficult to work with the Javanese Sukarno. They deliberately joined a nationalist organization based on the educated dedication of a few rather than the blind allegiance of many, as was the case for the party which Sukarno led. Sukarno's demagogy and the extremism of his programme, however, had the usual attraction. By mid 1933 he had some 20,000 members in his party. He was arrested in August of the same year and exiled. Hatta and Sjahrir (then a young man of twenty-five, about to return to the Netherlands) were next to be arrested, in February 1934. The government's repressive measures were successful in stifling the non-co-operative wing of Indonesian nationalism, but co-operation implied no greater confidence in the rulers.

Regrettably, the Dutch did nothing to decrease the distrust in which they were held. In mid 1936 the People's Council, biased towards Dutch interests though it was, passed a proposal that a conference be convened to discuss plans for self-government over a ten-year period. The government's negative attitude was already clear early in 1937, and the petition was formally rejected on 16 November 1938. It was hardly surprising that anti-Dutch and even anti-Western sentiments increased among the intelligentsia.

This was all the more unfortunate because Indonesia had thoroughly absorbed the Western way of life, at least in her higher circles. Except in the native principalities, there was no longer any national pattern of conduct. The same customs and habits were observed as in European households, even to the meals eaten.

Dutch repression had the effect of turning the eyes of Westernized Indonesians away from the West and towards Japan. That country's offer of autonomy to Korea in the mid thirties naturally made a very favourable impression. And though Japan's ambitions in Asia had become very clear, both Dutch and Indonesians were powerless and had learned only to distrust each other. Japan on the other hand was increasingly popular. Sympathy for her was a means of expressing antipathy towards the Dutch; in safer fashion than the more dangerous alternative of open hatred.

In May 1940 Holland was occupied by Nazi troops. The Indies government was then on its own, and knew that the Japanese were making plans for the conquest of the Indies. It might have been expected to reach some agreement with nationalist leaders and so obtain Indonesian support against the Japanese. But the Dutch proved to be gifted with no greater wisdom in danger than they had displayed in security.

At a conference held on 31 January 1941 Indonesian nationalists asked simply that an Indonesian be appointed a Lieutenant Governor-General; that Indonesians be appointed Assistant-Directors of the departments of administration; that several Indo-nesians be appointed to the Council of the Indies; that a Chamber of the People's Representatives be set up, to function as the House of Commons does in Britain, while the People's Council would act as the Senate; and that universal active and passive suffrage for both sexes be instituted. All that the Indies government agreed to do was set up a commission to study how to adapt the structure of the Netherlands Kingdom to the needs of the post-war era.

The Japanese attacked the Indies on 14 February 1942; the Allies surrendered three weeks later. The Dutch in the Indies having failed both to convince their articulate Indies subjects of the justice of their rule, and to ensure the economic stability of the country, had now proved unable to provide the first requirement of government: security against aggression.

8   Achievement of Independence

Occupation

INDONESIAN FREEDOM came into sight with the arrival of the
Japanese. The rapidity of their defeat of the Allies convinced even
the unlettered Indonesian that the European empire was not
eternal. But the Japanese also made many structural changes in
Indonesian society. Intentionally or not, these ensured that Dutch
rule would not return. All Europeans and most Eurasians were
quickly put into concentration camps. In the government service
this compelled the promotion of Indonesians, and ensured their grati-
tude, at least for the time being. Later disillusionment did not affect
the fact that the return of the Dutch would have meant demotion.
Lastly, it taught the extremist nationalists the technique of job-
creation by eviction which they were to practise some fifteen years
later, again against the Dutch.

The Japanese encouraged Indonesian nationalism, with the intention of using it for their own war aims. They permitted the flying of
the Indonesian flag and the playing of the Indonesian National
Anthem, both of which the Dutch had forbidden. They promised
the Indonesians self-government in the near future, and authorized
nationalist organizations. Sukarno was released from detention, and
a Central Advisory Board, a representative council for Indonesia,
was established with him as President. It was supposed to be
consulted before any important measures were drawn up. The
creation of similar local boards followed. Sukarno was given the
task of inducing the population to back the Japanese war effort: he

did so and preached nationalism at the same time. Equally important, the Japanese organized and trained a home guard, officered by Indonesians. It was intended for use against an Allied invasion; in the event it fought the Dutch, and became the backbone of the later Indonesian Army.

The Japanese attempted to enlist the fervent Muslims on their side by constituting an all-embracing Islamic organization. They also abolished the Dutch system of education and replaced it with a single unified type. The Indonesian language was developed and its use fostered all over the archipelago.

Other measures also encouraged the growth of a feeling of common nationality, though unintentionally. Where the Dutch had ruled indirectly and moderately, keeping themselves in the background, the harsh exactions of the Japanese aroused a common resentment. It provided fruitful soil for the propaganda being broadcast by the Indonesian nationalists over the wireless.

In brief, the Japanese occupation made Indonesians politically conscious, gave them a vested interest in opposition to Dutch rule, accustomed the nationalist leaders to political leadership, and provided them with military means of resistance. The Dutch, in contrast, offered much less. In December 1942 Queen Wilhelmina promised only a post-war reconstruction of the Kingdom 'with complete self-reliance and freedom of conduct for each part regarding its internal affairs';[5] there was no question of Indonesia for the Indonesians.

As the Japanese began losing the war, so they gave increased powers to Indonesians, and in October 1944 the Japanese Prime Minister promised them independence in the near future. Indonesian leaders were given greater freedom of action and Indonesians were appointed to responsible positions in the civil service. The decisive step came six months later when a committee with a large majority of Indonesians was set up to prepare for independence.

As the Allies won their battles, so Indonesian feeling turned against the Japanese, and a number of uprisings took place. On 6 August 1945 the first atomic bomb was dropped on Hiroshima, and Japan secretly offered to surrender. The next day the Japanese

Supreme Commander in Southeast Asia authorized the setting up of a committee to prepare the transfer of government to Indonesians. On 17 August, two days after Japan's unconditional surrender, Sukarno and Hatta declared Indonesia independent.

Revolution

However, many tribulations lay in store for the nationalists before their right to independence was acknowledged. They first had to throw off the Dutch. These were nowhere in sight when independence was declared, as the Netherlands had only just emerged from German occupation. The Allied forces in the region were British and American; but none were available to take over from the Japanese in the Indies until the end of September 1945. The six weeks' interregnum was invaluable to the Indonesians.

Immediately after independence was proclaimed, the Independence Preparatory Committee had approved a constitution for the new Republic of Indonesia, elected Sukarno President and Hatta Vice-President, set up twelve Ministries and approved a form of administration, together with a representative Nationalist Committee, a Nationalist Party, and a security force. Sukarno announced the composition of his cabinet in early September, and thereafter civilian government was taken over by the Republicans. The Japanese, completely demoralized by their defeat, and deprived of Allied control, took no steps to prevent the growth of Indonesian government organization, and helped or permitted the Indonesians to acquire arms and ammunition.

At the end of the month the first contingent of Allied troops arrived. For some time, perhaps since the Napoleonic Wars, Dutch control of the Indies had depended on British dominance in the Indian Ocean. In 1942 Dutch fate in the Indies had been sealed by the British loss of Singapore. So also now the Dutch sought the help of the British in helping them to recover their Empire, and when they failed, put the blame on the British (and Americans).

From the beginning of the Allied occupation of the Indies, British and Dutch views were opposed. The Dutch thought that the British ought to arrest Sukarno and his associates as Japanese collaborators.

The British felt that their task was not to reimpose Dutch authority on Indonesia, but only to rescue Allied prisoners of war and internees. They sought the co-operation of the Indonesian leaders and compelled the Dutch to negotiate with them. Following incidents between Indonesians and some Dutch contingents, further disembarkations of Dutch troops were stopped. Severe fighting between British troops and Indonesians at Surabaya in November 1945 convinced the Allies that the Republic was to be taken seriously.

Meanwhile, the Indonesians had abandoned the original presidential cabinet for a parliamentary one. In the same month Sjahrir emerged as Prime Minister. He was personally acceptable to the Dutch, whilst he sought to avoid war though adamantly refusing to recognize Netherlands sovereignty.

The Dutch now took account of their military and economic weakness, and consequent dependence on Britain. Under pressure, they committed themselves to granting Indonesian independence. Van Mook, the new Lieutenant Governor-General (no Governor-General was appointed after the war), suggested that the Republic be a partner in a Federal Indonesian Free State. The Indonesian reply was promising, but talks held with the government in the Netherlands were ineffectual. The Republican government thereafter refused all bilateral discussions with the Dutch and set about extending its international contacts.

Though the Dutch were not allowed to land on Java or Sumatra, from November 1945 their troops (drawn from former prisoners of war) reoccupied the other islands of the Indies and eventually took over control from the Australians there in July 1946. Immediately afterwards representatives of these islands conferred in the Celebes. They approved a federal structure for Indonesia, though they demanded its independence, and expressed the wish to maintain a special relationship between the Netherlands and Indonesia. One motive in their plans, it is fair to say, was a desire to dilute the Republic's strength in the independent Indonesia to which the Dutch were now committed.

Dutch troops were permitted on Java and Sumatra only in April 1946, when the British were making ready to go. Their approaching departure added urgency to the Dutch need to end the fighting with the Republicans. The result was the Linggadjati Agreement of November, which recognized the Republic as the *de facto* authority in Java and Sumatra. Both the Dutch and the Republic were to co-operate in forming a United States of Indonesia, which was to be sovereign, democratic, and federal; and a Netherlands-Indonesian Union, consisting of the Kingdom of the Netherlands and the United States of Indonesia, with the Queen of the Netherlands at its head.

The agreement only set out broad principles; each side therefore interpreted it to suit its own interests and acted accordingly. The Dutch set up puppet states: East Indonesia, West Borneo, and West Java, extended the area of their control and continued to blockade Republican ports. The Republicans, for their part, went on extending their foreign contacts. There were also violations of the cease-fire agreement, and Republican attempts to foment disorder and sabotage in East Indonesia.

The stalemate worked to the advantage of the extremists on either side, but it was ruinous to the Dutch Exchequer. The Republican area was self-sufficient; whilst the Dutch armed forces were a constant drain on Netherlands finances. The plantation areas, which would have replenished them, were outside the control of the Dutch, who held only the coastal areas of Java and Sumatra in addition to the other islands.

Consequently, in July 1947, Dutch troops invaded Republican territory, and so began the 'First Police Action', as it came to be called. Australia and India asked the Security Council to take immediate action to end hostilities. The Council called for a cease-fire, and set up a Good Offices Committee, whose members became Australia, Belgium, and the United States. The GOC brought the two parties together on the USN transport *Renville*, anchored in the harbour of Batavia, and agreement was reached in January 1948.

'Renville' provided that between six and twelve months from the signing of a political agreement, plebiscites supervised by the GOC would determine whether the various peoples of Indonesia wished to join the Republic or another state within the United States of Indonesia (USI). The Netherlands was to remain sovereign over Indonesia until the formation of the USI, within which the Republic was to be a State.

The Dutch flouted the agreement by conducting plebiscites in various parts of the archipelago, immediately and without GOC supervision. In March 1948 they announced a Provisional Federal Government consisting only of the Lieutenant Governor-General and his departmental heads, mostly Dutch; a state of affairs much as it was before the war.

The loss of territory suffered by the Republicans had caused economic privation for the people. The communists within the Republic gained strength, and in September 1948 attempted to seize power. They were suppressed only after two months bitter fighting.

Between the Republicans and the Dutch, matters grew steadily worse, and in December the Dutch began their 'Second Police Action'. They quickly captured Sukarno, Hatta, Sjahrir, and half of the Republican cabinet, who were flown to exile in Sumatra. The remaining Republican cities in both Java and Sumatra fell to the Dutch, but they were unable to control the countryside.

The world was shocked by the Dutch action. The US Economic Co-operation Administration suspended aid to the Netherlands Indies government. The Security Council called for an end to hostilities and a release of political prisoners, and increased the powers of the GOC, which it rechristened the United Nations Commission for Indonesia (UNCI), instructing it to act as the Council's representative in Indonesia.

Independence

Under the auspices of the UNCI an agreement between the Dutch and the Republicans was reached in May 1949. No small part had been played by the United States, who offered assistance to the Republicans if they reached agreement with the Dutch, and threatened the latter with economic penalties if they did not come to terms with the Indonesians. The Republicans agreed to take part in a Round Table Conference at The Hague to arrange the unconditional transfer of sovereignty to a United States of Indonesia. The Dutch in turn consented to end military operations, and to release all political prisoners.

In July of the same year representatives of the Dutch-created states, known as Federalists, who were now convinced that they had to find some accommodation with the Republicans, accepted that the sovereignty of the USI would be derived from the Republic as well as from the Netherlands, that the constituent states of the federation would not possess separate forces, and that the Republic's forces would form the nucleus of the Federal Army. They also undertook to support the Republic's demand for unconditional transfer of sovereignty, and for the territory it held at the time of 'Renville'. In return, the Republicans agreed that in the USI the fifteen Federal states set up by the Dutch would have two-thirds of the representation in the House of Representatives, whilst the Senate would have co-legislative powers with the House of Representatives in matters concerning the relations between the Central government and the component states, or in matters concerning the relations between the states; the Senate was to decide which matters fell into these categories; its decisions would be overridden only by a two-thirds majority in the House of Representatives.

A cease-fire was finally agreed between the Netherlands and the Republic in August 1949, and late in that month the Round Table Conference on the transfer of sovereignty began at The Hague. Three delegations took part: one from the Netherlands, one from the Republic, and one from the Federal states.

Under pressure from the United States, agreement was reached that sovereignty over the entire territory of the former Netherlands Indies, with the exception of Western New Guinea, would be transferred completely and unconditionally from the Netherlands to the Republic of the United States of Indonesia. This was to be a Federal government, formed of the Republic of Indonesia and of the fifteen political units established by the Dutch.

Also established was a Netherlands-Indonesian Union bearing certain similarities to the conventions of the British Commonwealth, and a Union Court to arbitrate differences between the two countries. Dutch troops were to be withdrawn in the shortest possible time after the transfer of sovereignty; Dutch economic rights and privileges were reaffirmed.

None of the preceding matters caused much dispute. What did were the questions of Indonesia's monetary debt to the Netherlands, and Western New Guinea. Neither of the Indonesian delegations was prepared to shoulder the costs of Dutch military actions against the Republic. Eventually they accepted a debt of 4,300 million guilders, 3,000 million being the internal debt (which included sums raised to finance the Dutch military effort against the Republic) and 1,300 million the external.

The Netherlands, with neither legal nor historical justification, refused to include Western New Guinea in the transfer of sovereignty. The Indonesian delegations were divided on the issue, with the Federalists determined on having the territory, the Republicans less so. For the Federalists, it was the evidence that their method of achieving independence, namely by co-operating with the Dutch, was as effective as the intransigence of the Republicans. Had they been successful, their hands would have been considerably strengthened, and the world would have been saved much trouble. The Republicans, on the other hand, were much more concerned to obtain sovereignty as quickly as possible. They saw clearly that the longer independence was delayed, the stronger would become the governments in the non-Javanese territories, and consequently the more difficult to dissolve or subdue after independence.

The UNCI eventually produced a face-saving formula whereby the final decision over the status of Western New Guinea was to be settled in discussions to take place in the ensuing year: on 27 December 1949 sovereignty was formally transferred. Batavia had its name changed to Djakarta, after the Jakatra which had stood on the same site before Coen had destroyed it three centuries earlier.

The federal structure of the new state was not to last. The predominantly Javanese Republicans had long been determined on a unitary constitution. Despite bloody opposition in East Indonesia, they achieved success by 17 August 1960, when the Republic of Indonesia came into being.

48 Railways were established by the Dutch at the end of the nineteenth century.

49 In 1916 certain powers were transferred from the Netherlands to the Indies and a *Volksraad* (People's Council) was set up.

50 Marxist ideas had begun to develop with the founding of the Indies Social Democratic Association in 1914.

51 The manufacture of textiles did not begin until the 1930s. A cloth market at Surakarta in Java.

52 Western influence upon Indonesia is reflected in this comparatively new housing estate.

53 The Japanese attacked and occupied Indonesia in 1942. The erection of a bridge in Java by the conquerors.

54 The Japanese encouraged nationalism and obtained sup-port against the Allies. They also formed an Indonesian-officered home guard, some of whose members here express their support.

55 As the Japanese began losing the Second World War, so they gave increased power to Indonesia. Eventually on 17 August 1945 President Sukarno (left) and Vice-President Hatta made a joint statement declaring independence.

56 After the proclamation of independence in 1945 a guerrilla force, or 'Laskar Kakyat', was formed.

57 Support for the new Republic of Indonesia was demonstrated throughout the country.

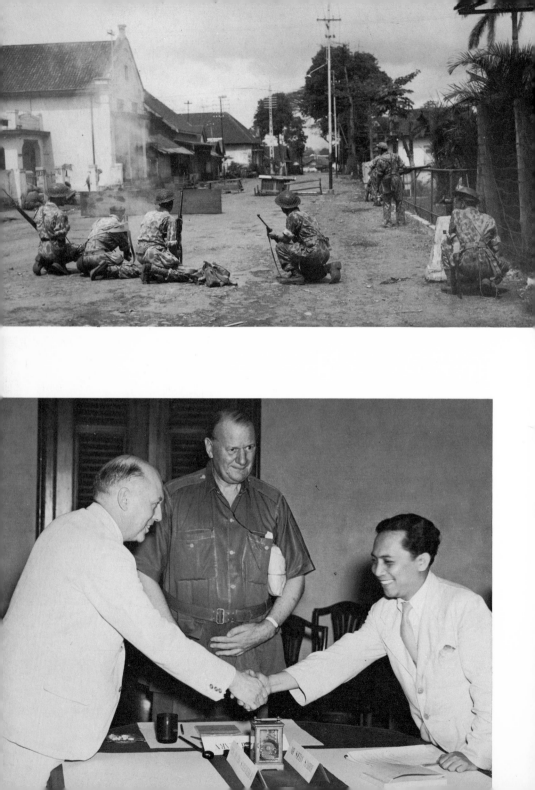

58 (*left above*) The Dutch tried to regain their empire and hostilities ensued against the Republicans.

59 (*left below*) A cease-fire was agreed in August 1949; Willem Schmerhorn (left) shakes hands with Sutan Sjahrir, the Indonesian representative, after a meeting chaired by Lord Killearn (centre).

60 A polling booth at Jogyakarta in Java during the election of 1955.

61 To help the illiterate majority make their choice, the parties adopted distinctive symbols.

62 No schools existed for Indonesians before 1854, and it was only when the Dutch government created the 'village' school in 1907 that progress was made. A primary school for Indonesians.

63 These were distinct from the school designed for the Dutch only. This is a typical Dutch kindergarten.

9   Social Personality

Urban Culture

THE TRANSFER OF SOVEREIGNTY marked the end of the fighting against the Dutch, but the beginning of the long and arduous task of creating a viable nation. For while Indonesia was now an independent state, very few of its people could be called 'Indonesian' in any true sense. The country was rather composed of very many different peoples, with little to bind them. Indeed, perhaps the only thing they had in common, and which distinguished them from the subjects of other states, was that they had once been under a Dutch administration centred on Batavia. Even then, as we have seen, their treatment had by no means been uniform.

A man may often be identified by the social institutions in which he participates, and which distinguish him from the people outside them. Those in Indonesia, however, do not for the most part embrace all the country's citizens, but only certain groups. Some institutions are fairly uniform throughout the archipelago; others differ from one local community to another. The former may be called Western institutions, more or less changed in the Indonesian environment. These enfold very few people indeed, but their numbers are growing with the spread of Western education, even though their Westerniza⁄ tion is simultaneously being diluted by local influences. It is this group which to a greater or lesser extent is engaged in employment of a Western type, and which attempts to follow a Western style of life. Many of its members, particularly the older ones, speak Dutch well; the younger ones increasingly are mastering English. They see Western films, they wear Western clothes; they look forward to a material standard of living not radically different from that prevailing in the West. (Such is the climate of opinion in Indonesia that the term Western is rarely used; rather it is substituted by the word 'modern'.)

This is, very generally speaking, the culture of the apex of the social scale, the culture associated with the towns. This is not to say that everybody in the towns is Westernized, but that the Westernized are found in the towns rather than the villages; though many, perhaps most, in the towns are not Westernized. It is the towns which are considered modern and refined, and the abode of the upper classes; the rural is coarse, old-fashioned, and the home of the lower orders.

The division between urban and rural is often largely coincidental with that between educated and uneducated. As early as the end of the nineteenth century the intelligentsia began to be accepted by the aristocracy, even though they were of common birth. Nowadays, the same prestige attaches to education, and is buttressed by many factors. First, the scanty opportunities for higher education under the Dutch meant that when independence was achieved, those few well educated held all power in their hands. (It has been estimated that in 1958 as few as 2,000 people made all the important decisions in Indonesia.[6]) When it came to devising rules for the civil service, the new rulers followed the example of the Dutch and made promotion dependent on the level of education reached.

In the past the upper classes were the aristocracy, who lived in Court towns (such as Jogyakarta and Surakarta in Java), and the nobility, who lived in smaller towns modelled on the larger. This well-born group were known, in Java, as the *priyayi*, and were considered to be the repository of Courtly manners and of refinement. Of course, as in most parts of the world, the refined did not work with their hands.

The priyayi are no longer in positions of power, and do not constitute an upper class (not, at least, on grounds of their birth). The new upper classes make claims to privilege quite other than descent, though many of their members are of priyayi origin, and still bear the appropriate titles. One element they continue to retain, however, in common with the priyayi: service to the state. They consist of senior officials, officers in the armed forces, senior staff of the large corporations, academic staff of the universities and other tertiary educational establishments (which are state institutions), officials of religion, doctors, lawyers, engineers, architects, politicians, writers and, generally, the intelligentsia; and, lastly, the new business group. Though the latter's profession is not regarded as deserving much prestige, nevertheless, it enables them to afford a Western way of life, which itself carries prestige. To be precise, what is admired is the ability to acquire the manufactured products of the West, from sun-spectacles to gold watches, typewriters, transistor radios and, of course, motor-cars. Such innovations as Western ballroom dancing, which go against custom, however, are much more contentious.

What are the means to and symbols of success in this sector of Indonesian society? To put it in another way, what kind of young man does a mother with a marriageable daughter look for? The first criterion is certainly education, but it is doubtful if by itself this is enough; it must also be seen to be propelling its possessor along the road to success. Just as important are family ties; a priyayi is infinitely preferable to a commoner, if only because he will almost certainly be well connected to those in positions of power and influence. The fourth criterion is that common to all societies: money. The larger the salary the young man is drawing, the richer his father, the more acceptable he is. Then comes ability; only placed last because if it has not borne fruit in education and wealth, it will not be highly regarded (the Javanese language, for instance, makes no distinction between 'stupid' and 'uneducated'). A person who has neither birth nor wealth nor education can also attain recognition if he can organize an association or a political party, making himself its chair-man or secretary. He then has to be deferred to by those in power, for fear of the damage he might do.

In addition to the upper class, there is also a middle class in the towns, composed mainly of clerks, petty traders, and manual labourers. These would be considered 'low people' but not 'peasants'. They would certainly not be considered refined, but neither would they *a priori* be considered coarse (by the refined, be it understood).

They are midway between the modern and the old-fashioned; probably in modern (at least not traditional) occupations themselves, but not doing very 'modern' work nevertheless. And the clerks, being necessarily educated, would be placed higher than the petty traders; and these, probably because of their greater earnings, would be placed higher than the manual labourers.

Village Institutions

One must, however, keep in mind that those who participate in a truly urban culture are very few. The largest cities and towns in Indonesia are Djakarta, Surabaya, Bandung, and Semarang in Java; and Medan and Palembang in Sumatra. In 1961 their combined population amounted to 6·4 million people; only about 6½ per cent of the population. Most Indonesians live in villages; this was, and in many places still is, a community whose members are jointly responsible for common welfare and public order. In Indonesian thinking the village is in the first place the community; the land, houses, and so forth that it owns are secondary. This mode of thought dates back to the time when there was a shortage of people, not of land, and what was important was people to work the land not, as now, land that people could work.

The community had the right of disposal over the fields, the adjacent forests, and uncultivated land. Those members of the community who had by their own efforts brought tracts of land under cultivation gained a personal right to these particular fields, subject to the community's prerogative to dispose of them in the common interest. In some parts of Indonesia, especially West Java, this limited claim to property developed into full ownership. In others, it disappeared altogether. This took place especially in Central Java, where communities were grouped together into larger units under hereditary rulers, who became the sole and absolute proprietors of all land.

Throughout Indonesia certain features of the original social organization still remain. Members of the community remain responsible for the common welfare. This includes the obligation to help one another in time of distress. In addition, they are expected to bear jointly the responsibility for crimes and offences committed in the village if the actual culprits are not discovered. This is abhorrent to the Western mind, and indeed the Dutch and after them the Indonesians have tried to introduce the notion of individual responsibility. But the village headman still remains a most influential person; and without his co-operation the government can do little. He is always selected from among members of the village; which is not the case for wider units. He is elected, not in the sense of being voted for, but rather in the sense of being agreed upon as the guardian of tradition.

Even within this stronghold of rural values, there are distinctions. They rest on two main criteria: length of residence in the village and amount and type of land held. Those who are granted the highest status are the descendants of the original colonists, probably an offshoot from some other, overpopulated village. Land-holdings are classified into food-producing and household land; the highest status is accorded to those who have the former and, of course, those who have most of it. Within the category of food-producing land, the highest prestige is given to paddy-fields (perhaps because they are the most productive); hill-side land used for growing crops holds a lower valuation.

A really substantial villager would therefore firstly be a descendant of the original colonists; secondly, he would hold considerable quantities of paddy-land, as well as probably some hill-side land, and certainly enough land on which a substantial house could be built, with a fair-sized yard. It would not be surprising to find such a person the head of the village.

But even in the village, urban values count. Those with the highest status are also those who have most urban contacts. Further, the wealth they have is converted into patronage; so that a man's status can often be measured by the number of dependents he has.

If the culture of the towns may be described as 'Westernism' or 'modernism', the oldest culture at village level, which is found throughout the archipelago, may be described as animism. Since 80 per cent of the Indonesian population lives in villages, the importance of animism needs no emphasis, especially as the function of religion in the village is mainly of social control; this is much more important than its philosophy. At the village level animistic beliefs and practices are very similar throughout Indonesia, whether among those peoples who acknowledge Islam, or among the Hindu-Buddhists of Bali, or among the Christian communities scattered through the islands. This does not imply, however, that such beliefs are exclusively Indonesian, nor that they have the same force all over the country.

These animistic basic beliefs, briefly, are those in a cosmic order, in the sanctity of ancestors, and in spirits. The first implies that all aspects of life are governed by supernatural forces; each person has his place in the whole; and it is essential to maintain harmony within the life pattern. On the other hand, however, ancestors are not worshipped, but simply revered; the practice of keeping up their graves is widespread throughout the archipelago. The belief in spirits is closely related to the reverence of ancestors; together they emphasize the unity of the group.

Some spirits are good, others are bad; it is the function of religious practices to keep these spirits in harmony; and as communal action is necessary to that end, communal solidarity acquires a religious sanction. Spirits are to be found in almost all inanimate objects, whether in forces of nature such as winds, mountains, volcanoes, or in daggers, gongs, drums. The spiritual value of an object is enhanced if it is ancient and has been passed on as an heirloom; there is an obvious link here with the reverence due to ancestors. But the most powerful spirits are to be found in animate beings, and animals are kept or shunned because of their spiritual qualities. Magical thinking is prominent; deer meat is not eaten, for example, for fear of assimilating the anxiety characteristic of the animal.

It is the human being, however, who carries most spiritual power. Some possess it in greater measure than others; these are the shamans, priests, mediums, or diviners. Their power is usually much respected; sometimes it is greatly feared. It is also believed possible to gain power over another human being by obtaining his hair or nail clippings; sometimes it is thought that knowledge of another person's name can be used in a similar way; hence names are in some places closely guarded secrets. Also, in Java for instance, names may be changed to bring good luck. A person who can win spiritual potency from others naturally becomes power-laden. Among most Indonesian peoples the king or leader was considered spiritually powerful; and his descent was usually traced back to one or another deity who founded the royal line. This of course encouraged usurpers to manufacture similar genealogies for themselves.

The spirits of the living are clearly distinguished from those of the dead. The latter are generally unwelcome, best confined to graves. They are not, however, considered evil; the Javanese, for instance, go to their ancestors' graves at all important places of the life-cycle. But precautions are taken to ensure that the spirit of a recently dead person actually does go to the burial-place. Neither life after death nor reincarnation into other lives are clearly developed ideas.

The various aspects of spirit worship described above are to be found throughout Indonesia, and not exclusively in the villages. It is not uncommon for highly Westernized professional men to turn to older relatives versed in these basic beliefs, to learn the propitious dates for such important events as, say, moving house. Animistic practices may, therefore, be considered the most truly Indonesian institutions, provided 'Indonesian' is not taken in an exclusive sense. But nowhere do they exist alone; in most of the area one or other of the great world religions has penetrated, though not to the extent of having its adherents abandon all their previous practices.

Islam

After the animist, the most widespread institutions are those of Islam; over 90 per cent of the population profess the religion. The reader should not assume that the Islamic beliefs and practices of Indonesia are identical with those of other Islamic countries. Just as, say, Roman Catholicism in England is not identical with that practised in Italy, so also Islam in Indonesia has been strongly affected by the beliefs and practices which existed before its adoption. These differ from place to place; in Java particularly, as we know, Islam was preceded by Hinduism and Buddhism. In consequence, Islam in Indonesia is not only different from Islam in the Middle

East, but also varies between Java and the other islands. In Indonesia, as elsewhere, the sea unites, the land divides, and the coastal Muslim communities often have more in common with one another than with their fellow-believers inland.

Since Java holds most of the Indonesian population, and Islam was there preceded by Hinduism and Buddhism, we may consider what now remains of those beliefs. The reader will remember that Hinduism began to arrive in the archipelago about the second century A.D., that Mahayana Buddhism followed before the eighth century A.D., but very quickly achieved a *modus vivendi* with Hinduism, and that after A.D. 1000 the two religions amalgamated into a single form of religious expression. Hindu-Buddhism's day was done, however, by A.D. 1500, when the last Javanese Hindu-Buddhists fled to Bali before the Muslims.

It seems that Hinduism agreed with Indonesian animistic beliefs. The rice spirit remains identified with the Hinduistic *Dewi Sri* and the spirit of death as *Durga*. A very widespread institution originating from Hinduism is the shadow play (*wayang kulit*), which depicts stories from the *Ramayana* and the *Mahabharata*. The behaviour so pictured still remains the Javanese ideal of comportment. It is quite likely that these shadow plays served as a link, for which there is no later substitute, between all levels of the Javanese social order.

At present only Bali, part of Lombok, and small enclaves in Central and West Java profess Hinduism. Balinese Hinduism shows a certain mixture with Buddhism (as did late Javanese Hinduism), and has of course been modified by the previous patterns of life, so that only about 6 per cent of the Balinese are in a Hinduistic caste system. The others are the villagers, who are outside the Hinduistic religious and state structure. In consequence the Hinduism of Bali has only a very slight similarity to that of India.

Whereas in Java Islam had been preceded by Hinduism, in most of the other islands of the archipelago, where the Hindu impress had not been so deep, it laid its foundations directly on the animistic beliefs and practices of the inhabitants.

Coming from India, Islam had been much influenced by pan-theism and mysticism, as we have seen, and was to that extent more palatable to the Indonesians. The spread of Islam, after the collapse of Madjapahit, proceeded so rapidly that the finer points of doctrine were often overlooked, and what resulted was mainly a nominal allegiance to what appeared to be the newly successful ideology. Reform movements from Mecca in the late eighteenth century tried to purge Indonesian Islam of much of its mystical content, but the pre-Islamic life patterns remained. These reform movements were, however, an attempt to return to orthodoxy. In the late nine-teenth century the reform movements were of Islamic modernism, which attempted to rid Indonesian Islam of both local and historical 'excrescences'. And today the fight continues, between orthodox Indonesian Islam, with its local and historical beliefs, and modernist Islam, shorn of both.

Islam is an all-embracing religion; it does not limit itself to a sphere called 'religious', and in fact acknowledges no divisions, as are made in the West, between religion, politics, economics, and so forth. Its law (the *Shari'ah*) is theoretically supposed to regulate all aspects of life, though this ideal has never been attained. This law has two main foundations, the Koran or *Qur'an*, the message of God as revealed through his Prophet Muhammad, compiled several years after his death in A.D. 632; and the Hadith, or Tradition, which enshrines the traditions concerning Muhammad's life, and is a guide to what Muslims should do. With the spread of Islam, interpreta-tions arose to guide the faithful in local situations, and soon became organized into schools. That followed by Indonesians is the *Shafi'ite*.

For the majority of Indonesians, Islam means certain religious ceremonies and duties; the political and juridical aspects concern them little. These ceremonies and duties deal with the individual's relation to God, and are known as the Five Pillars, as set forth by Muhammad. The first pillar is: the affirmation of Faith (*shahadat*), 'I testify that there is no god but God, and that Muhammad is his prophet.' Every Muslim must say this at least once during his lifetime, and if said in good faith makes the individual a Muslim, although most, but not all, Muslim communities also insist on circumcision.

The second pillar is prayer, known in Indonesia as *sembahyang* or *salat*. Islam enjoins it five times a day; the extent to which this rule is followed in Indonesia varies considerably and shows an inverse association with the degree of Hinduization. The least zealous are therefore the Javanese of Central and East Java; those less affected by Hinduization, such as the Sundanese and Bantamese people of West Java or the Menangkabau of West Central Sumatra, or the Atjehnese of Atjeh, are all more fervent.

Islam's third pillar is fasting. Certain days and months of the Islamic year are set aside for it; the greatest is the whole of the ninth month known as *Puasa* in Indonesia. By comparison with North Africa, Indonesia's support of this pillar is very lax. The fast ends with a great feast known as *lebaran* (*bairam* in other parts of the Muslim world) or *Id ul Fitri*, which also coincides with the Javanese calendar's New Year. On this day Indonesians visit graves, elder relatives, and friends. The younger ask the older for forgiveness of their sins by omission or commission during the preceding year.

Charity is the fourth pillar. The giving of tithes, known as *zakat* in Indonesia, is the most important duty of good Muslims in this respect. Most commonly, tithes are levied on the rice harvest. In addition, a special tax known as *pitrah* is levied at the end of the fasting month; it takes the form of food and money, and is destined for the relief of the poor and orphans.

The fifth and last pillar of Islam is the pilgrimage to Mecca, known as the *hadj*, and is taken most seriously in Indonesia. It occurs during the last month of the Muslim year, and every adult Muslim is expected to make the pilgrimage once. Those who go on pilgrimage tend to come from the better-off sections of the peasantry. It is increasingly rural-based; urban-dwellers are losing their fascination for the pilgrimage.

Though over 90 per cent of the Indonesian population are professed Muslims, many refer to themselves as *Islam statistik* (Muslim for statistical purposes). Indeed, in those parts of Java, where the orthodox Muslims are most strongly entrenched, the people describe themselves as *santri*, if they are fervent (and, frequently, with a vested interest in the Muslim religious organization), and *abangan* if they are more inclined to the traditional animistic beliefs and practices veneered by Islam.

This distinction between santri and abangan, however, is quite ignored by the nobility or priyayi (see above), who pride themselves on being the repository of Javanese-Hindu-Buddhist culture, with only a perfunctory nod at Islam. Commoners might or might not become fervent Muslims, and in consequence might or might not abandon their animistic practices, but the priyayi look on all this from a great height. Not that some of them do not become santri, but when they do so they abandon the culture of the priyayi.

Within the pious Islamic community itself there is, as we have implied, a deep schism between the orthodox and the modernists. The modernists, like reformers in other religions, reject the various interpretations of the original holy books, and accept the authority of only the Koran and Hadith. They argue that in this way Islam will retain its purity and still be able to accept the learning of the West.

It is important to observe, however, that the division between orthodox and modernists, though it is partly doctrinal, has also its ethnic and political connotations. The orthodox are almost exclusively to be found in Central and East Java, especially the latter, and are most strongly supported by the rural population. Their political representation lies in the Nahdatul Ulama Party. The modernists, on the other hand, gain much of their support either from urban dwellers in Java or from the islands other than Java. They found their social representation in the movement known as the Muhammadiyah, and their political in the Masjumi Party, suppressed in 1959.

Ethnic groupings represent a further narrowing of the process of identification of an Indonesian. His Westernism he shares with many other peoples, both near and far; equally his Islam. But his Western-ism-Islam combination, on the other hand, distinguishes him more than either characteristic separately, while, say, Westernist-Muslim-Javanese culture identifies him yet further.

As we have seen in Chapter 1, the Javanese are much the largest of the ethno-linguistic groups; it is also fair to say that their culture is the most complex, at least in part due to the fact that they absorbed the greatest amount of influence from Hindu-Buddhism. Given their preponderance, their values (which are the best known) are of some significance. These originated in peasant society, and have of course been much modified in the towns.

The first value of importance (throughout the archipelago incidentally) is loyalty to kinship ties, which provide security and welfare for the whole family. In consequence, that form of social organization is considered desirable which models itself on the family or wider kin group. Furthermore, no Indonesian either desires or dares to deny the claims of kinship on him; hence nepotism in public life. Often, this is simply a return for the sacrifices his family and kin group have made to qualify him for his position. Indonesians also tend to assimilate their other relationships to those within the family; so that elders are addressed by the term for 'father'. In addition, friends, once accepted, are treated as brothers or sisters. Naturally, therefore, Indonesians do not make friends easily; and friendships between adolescent boys and girls are proscribed.

Another set of Javanese values are drawn from peasant society. Prominent among them is the idea of mutual aid, or *gotong royong*. In isolated villages exclusively dependent on agriculture, mutual aid still accomplishes many of the necessary tasks. Perhaps for the very good reason that to pay workers for all the necessary development tasks would make the inflation worse than it already is, Indonesia emphasizes gotong royong in national life, as also it does co-operatives as agencies for trade.

Like most traditional cultures the world over, Javanese culture places great value upon respect for elders and, closely allied with it, obedience to authority. This applies within the family as within the wider society. Resistance to authority may be expressed only through passive refusal to obey, or through complete withdrawal from the situation or, in desperation, rebellion. In turn, the means of re-establishing authority is hardly ever one of pitiless chastisement of the offender, but rather one of compromise, in order to permit social harmony to be restored. This value of obedience is in turn supported by the counterpart duty of the elder or authorities to provide for those in his or their charge.

Perhaps also deriving from village society, where people are compelled to live with one another whatever their feelings, is the value of toleration. But this has fairly narrowly circumscribed limits. While the Indonesian will willingly grant the right of other religions, for instance, to coexist, he will not tolerate a religion which threatens to exterminate his. His tolerance in turn is supported by another value: the avoidance of open disagreement. As perhaps in most societies, the best solution is one where no party loses face. Disagreement must be expressed only in indirect fashion.

Both tolerance and the avoidance of open disagreement call for self-restraint. This value, which the Javanese prize in common with older complex societies the world over, requires that a gentleman should neither talk too much, nor be opinionated, nor laugh too loud, nor gesture excessively. His feelings he must keep to himself; all he can show is dignity and self-respect. The other societies of Indonesia, which have never developed an aristocratic structure, prize these virtues very much less.

Other values related to village life are the lack of a real sense of time or of its value; and in consequence there is no planning of future activities. Work is not considered as desirable in itself, but as something that must be done. On the other hand, however, work and leisure are not separated; these categories of thought are unknown to the Javanese villager. And the product of work, wealth, is to be shared. This does not mean a communistic egalitarianism, but rather provision for the less fortunate. Traditionally, the use of private property was subject to social controls, but severe inroads are now being made into this prescription. Nevertheless, Indonesian employers still take a paternalistic interest in the welfare of their employees, whilst foreign firms are forced to provide rice and clothing. So long has the village been at the mercy of either nature or tyrants, that fatalism and passivity have assumed the role of major values in the culture. The idea that man can change his fate is new, though gaining ground.

As in the other cultures of Southeast Asia, and in great contrast with India or China, women enjoy a very high status. So much is this so that the Islamic prescriptions for divorce have had to be adjusted to customary law in this respect, virtually giving women the same rights of divorce as men. Paradoxically, in a relative sense woman's status has been highest among the villagers. Among the upper classes she tended to be, for public purposes at least, subordinate to the man. Feminism in Indonesia has done much to liberate her.

In certain respects, however, Javanese values are opposed to those held by the other groups. Whilst their courtly culture regards service to the monarch or the state as the occupation carrying most prestige, and despises trade, the values of the other peoples are no-where near as inimical to this latter occupation. The Javanese were long centralized; the other peoples lived in fairly small democratic communities; their feeling of equality and esteem for initiative are much greater than those of the Javanese. They have, of course, the usual concomitant of an egalitarian social structure, namely coarser manners; Javanese are much more refined. However, one conse-quence is that the less a culture has been influenced by Java, the more readily it takes to economic development; another is that it is very difficult for the Javanese and the others to agree either on goals or on the means to pursue them.

The affiliation with an ethnic group may be identified in various ways. For instance, most Javanese have peculiarly Javanese names; only a minority has opted for the Islamic names which they share with their fellow-Indonesians. Those who have are mostly the fervent, or santri. Also, dress differs; though most Indonesian women, and some men, wear the wrap-around skirt known as the *kain* its colouring distinguishes the various peoples. Physical frame and skin colouring also vary between the ethnic groups; while each has its own food preparations, musical styles, and forms of artistic expression. All this is not to deny that from the point of view of the anthropologist, there is a fundamental unity of culture among all Indonesians (though it may well also include the Malays); neverthe-less, the individual member of a group may be more aware of his differences from other groups than his similarities to them.

Customs differ between the groups. To take one example, a basic Javanese custom, the *selamatan*, is little known outside Java. This is a ritual repast given by an individual or family for almost any life crisis; i.e. pregnancy, birth, circumcision, marriage, etc. Male neigh-bours and relatives are invited; the host gives the reason for the repast, and asks that the good spirits allow matters to proceed normally. A mosque official recites a prayer in Arabic, and on occasion the host may also beseech Hindu gods. The food is then distributed to those present. The guests eat a little, then wrap up the remainder and take it home to their families. Selamatans are also held at various critical phases of the growing of rice, at the construction of a new house, and before or after a journey. Some modernist Muslim leaders condemn this practice.

Within each ethnic group there are of course smaller units with which the individual identifies himself, and again these are not the same for all. Some of the peoples have a unilineal structure, i.e. they trace their descent through one or other side of the family, and are organized into groups on that basis. For instance, the Menangkabau of Central Sumatra trace their descent through the female side of the family, and traditionally live in long-houses where the connexion is traced through the female line. Property is also inherited through that line, and so is authority, though it is exercised by men.

Most of the peoples, however, including the numerous Javanese, recognize both sides of the family, and naturally the nuclear family tends to be found living alone (it would be rather difficult to have senior relatives of both lines living under the same roof or in the same compound). The allegiance is not to a line of blood relatives, but rather to all those living in what is considered the same place. For practical purposes, this means the village, though the more intimate link is with the hamlet, and within that, with the neighbourhood association. Especially is this the case where what were 'natural' villages have been grouped together into a new village for adminis-trative reasons, and degraded to hamlets.

In brief, therefore, the social description of an Indonesian requires two sets of criteria. The first group one may consider as 'horizontal' because they run over all, or much, of the archipelago. They are Westernism and Islam. These are not alternative categories; though a person may be exclusively either Westernized, or a fervent Muslim, modernist or orthodox, he may also be a Westernized Muslim. The point here is that a Westernized person from one part of the archi-pelago will be able to make immediate contact with a Westernized person from another part of the archipelago; he might not with a villager even from his own part. The same may be said about the Muslim; the degree of his fervour, either orthodox or modernist, will measure the extent of his entry into a certain system of com-munication which stretches all over the archipelago (and, like Westernism, beyond).

The vertical divisions are typically those of ethnic groups, or regions, or villages. An Indonesian's behaviour represents the propor-tions of the horizontal and the vertical criteria in him. The Western-ized Javanese and the Westernized Menangkabau are both Muslim, but their ethnic differences remain extremely important. And, of course, when ethnic divisions coincide with religious distinctions, as between the Muslim Javanese and Christian Ambonese, there is little in common. The error is to assume *a priori* that a Westernized Indonesian has shed his family or ethnic links, or his animistic background, or his Islam. These all exist in him, in varying degrees, together with his Westernism; it is the mixture of them all that makes him what he is.

10   The Economy

Aims

ONE OF INDONESIA'S GREATEST NEEDS has been to make her economy productive. It is true that the Western traders (Muslim, Portuguese, English, Dutch) had brought Indonesia into the world market, and her people had undoubtedly produced more as a result. But as time went on they became too dependent on the world market for their own good. The great crash of 1929 had shown how vulnerable the economy had become. Also, as a result of the difficulty of adjusting supplies of agricultural products to fluctuations in prices, Indonesia was at a great disadvantage compared with the industrialized nations, and had found that over time more and more produce had to be given for the same quantity of manufactured goods.

Furthermore, it had become clear that peasant agriculture, as practised in Indonesia, was no longer able to provide a decent life for the people. Improvements in land productivity by such means as irrigation, fertilizers, etc., had failed to match the growth in population which they, and improved hygiene, encouraged. Only by increasing the amount of manufacturing in the country could surplus people be made productive; the growth of population might thereby be matched and even retarded. Quite apart from the economic arguments, of course, there was a strong political urge to become an industrialized nation like others in the modern world.

On attaining independence, therefore, Indonesia was faced with the task of not only repairing the neglect and destruction of war, occupation, and revolution, but also of changing the basis of the economy. As well as the need to improve agricultural productivity, it was also necessary to diversify the range of primary produce offered to the world market, so that falls in the price of any one product would not have too serious an effect on the economy as a whole. In addition, imports had to be replaced as much as possible by local manufacturing.

To judge how Indonesia has succeeded in achieving these objectives, we shall consider first her agricultural and industrial resources; then the foreign aid she has received in addition; thirdly, her plans on how to use these resources; and last, her performance.

Food Crops

Four out of five Indonesians are on the land, occupying an average of only half an acre each; and the earth is not rich. As in other tropical areas with heavy rainfall, the soluble substances are washed out of the soil, and most of the Indonesian islands are infertile and have sparse populations. The exceptions are Java, where volcanic activity exposes new fertile material at the surface, so counteracting the effects of rain, and a few other places, such as Central and South Sumatra and southwest Celebes. In consequence, unlike the other islands, Java bears the greatest density of population and has very little forest left.

In the fertile and densely populated areas mentioned the staple foodstuff, rice, is grown in flooded fields, known as *sawah*. This is a labour-intensive method of cultivation with a yield higher than can be obtained in dry farming (though far lower than in Japan). The main tools used in the flooded rice-fields are ploughs, harrows, and hoes. All originally were of wood, but now have iron and steel parts. Ploughs and harrows are still basically wooden; the hoe now has an iron blade with a steel core. The draught animals are water-buffalo and oxen. Planting and weeding are done manually, all or in part by women and children, as is harvesting in Java. Most of the rice is pounded at home, but some goes to modern mills.

Outside the fertile areas the common practice is a technique of shifting cultivation, which consists of clearing a plot of virgin forest and burning the felled trees. The land is usually fertile and, in fact, gives a higher yield than the Javanese sawah. After a few years' cultivation, however, the soil is exhausted, and the people move on. Left alone for about ten years, the forest will recover. If, however, as is increasingly the case, population pressure compels burning the forest earlier, grasses will take root and prevent its further use.

In Java *tegalan* (dry fields) are also cultivated, watered only by rain. If this is copious, they may be planted with rice. The yields are of course lower than in the case of the irrigated field. The most important of the subsidiary food crops, maize and cassava, are grown in these dry fields. The former is the staple food in the Lesser Sunda islands; elsewhere, both are eaten in addition to rice. Maize ripens more rapidly than cassava, and is therefore preferred as a second crop. In East Java and Madura, the centre of cattle rearing, it is widely produced as feed. Cassava is easily grown, but has low nutritional value; only in very poor districts does it form the main diet. Other dry-field crops of some importance are soya, green beans, ground-nuts, sweet potatoes, egg plant, and red peppers, an essential ingredient in Indonesian cooking.

The average holding in Java is only 1·9 acres per family, of which 0·8 acre is sawah, and 1·1 acres is dry field and garden compound, including house and stable. This size of holding permits only subsistence farming; nothing is left over for improvements. There is little land that can be set aside for commercial crops, and the peasant cannot afford fertilizers or better equipment, and rarely better seed. He uses his own labour intensively, but this is not enough to keep him busy all the time. Hence there is much disguised unemployment ('under-employment'), relieved only by the fact that several members of the family occupy themselves with handicrafts, horticulture, keeping livestock, work on adjacent plantations in season; in brief, anything to supplement family income.

There is, therefore, much excess labour of great inefficiency and immobility. So when prices fall, the smallholder works more, rather than less, to maintain his family. He dare not take risks or specialize in one cash crop, as this is subject to price fluctuations. When he cultivates a cash crop, he does so carelessly; it is not his prime concern. Left to himself, it is unlikely that he will break out of the cycle of inefficiency and consequent poverty.

Cash Crops

Nearly all Indonesia's cash crops are produced by both smallholders and estates. Some, however, come mainly from smallholders; others mainly from estates. In the first category fall rubber, copra, sugar, and coffee. In the second are tea and tobacco. Broadly speaking, where a crop requires constant attention, it is produced mainly on estates. Palm-oil is exclusively an estate product because of the complicated processing which is necessary; while pepper is grown only by small-holders.

Rubber was first introduced into Indonesia by large estates shortly after it was successfully planted in Malaya at the beginning of this century. Smallholders soon took it up as it is easy to cultivate, thrives in warm coastal plains up to about 4,500 feet in altitude, can grow in indifferent soils and stand considerable neglect, and is not easily killed by careless tapping. The smallholder can tap when prices are high, and turn to other crops when they are low. His problems emerge when the time comes to replant. When prices are high, he prefers to tap; when they are low, he cannot afford to replant. This is where the estates score.

As against about 1 million smallholders on a total of 3,200,000 acres, there are about 700 to 950 estates on about 1,300,000 acres mostly in Sumatra, principally on the northeast coast. About two-thirds of the smallholders are to be found on that island also, with the remainder on Kalimantan (Indonesian Borneo).

Copra, the dried meat of the coconut, is the next most important agricultural export product after rubber. In the home economy it is the principal source of frying-oil. The tree itself is used in the build-ing of houses, for matting, baskets, etc. It can grow anywhere in the archipelago from water's edge up to 2,000 feet, and thrives best on light and porous soil. Good land is not used for it, however, as the yield per acre is low in value.

Java provides near-ideal conditions for the growing of sugar-cane. The soil is good, and the centre and east of the island have the necessary dry season. The water it needs when growing is provided by extensive irrigation systems. The smallholders use a high-yielding variety developed before the Second World War.

The coffee plant is found mainly in Sumatra. Its cultivation is never a full-time occupation for the smallholders; when the world price falls the smallholder turns to rice. The estates, as usual, work on more scientific lines. They select suitable sites and, unlike the smallholders, prepare the soil and fertilize, drain, and weed it.

In the cultivation of tea, labour is the paramount consideration, as the plant needs constant care, and the leaves are picked continuously. Hence it is not grown in sparsely settled areas, but rather on the hill-sides of West and East Java and West Sumatra.

Labour requirements are perhaps even more important in the case of tobacco, which requires very intensive cultivation. Most of the estates are located in Deli (East Sumatra), Central Java, and parts of East Java. Smallholders also are to be found in Central and East Java.

Pepper is cultivated mainly in South Sumatra, the island of Bangka, and West Kalimantan. Though very profitable, its highly specific requirements of soil and climate limit its cultivation.

Manufacture

Industrialization requires certain essential ingredients. Prominent among them are entrepreneurial ability, raw materials, and capital.

Indonesia's domestic entrepreneurial resources, on attaining independence, consisted of Chinese and Eurasians. But to ensure that Indonesians acquired control of the economy, the Eurasians were first repressed and then expelled; whilst the Chinese were also hindered and then evicted from the rural areas. At the same time the government provided incentives for Indonesians to assume entrepreneurial functions. The only result was to bring into being a class of Indonesian 'front-men', in whose names the firms were registered, but who devolved their entrepreneurial functions on to 'back-room' Chinese. Few entrepreneurs were created.

Industrial raw materials are not substantial in Indonesia. Coal production runs at about 500,000 metric tons per annum: most of it sold for transportation fuel. Good coking coal is so scarce that it can support a steel industry with an annual capacity of only 150,000 metric tons.

Much industrial energy, throughout the world, is obtained from petroleum, and Indonesia has often been considered a major source of oil deposits. However, government policy towards foreign oil companies long prevented any exploration after independence. Happily, in June 1963 agreement was reached with the major companies operating in Indonesia (Shell, Caltex, and Stanvac), and exploration began the next year.

Indonesia's supplies of iron-ore are not large, they are widely distributed geographically, and the iron content of the ore is relatively low. It has been calculated that any steel industry would have a maximum capacity of only 5,400,000 metric tons.

With regard to other minerals, good deposits of bauxite have been reported in the Riau archipelago and in North Sumatra, and an aluminium industry seems quite possible, using power from a hydro-electric project at Asahan in North Sumatra when it is completed. Deposits of tin, copper, manganese, and a few other minerals are also to be found. Tin, indeed, is one of Indonesia's most valuable exports.

In brief, it is unlikely that Indonesia will be able to develop heavy industries. The chances for consumer goods industries are better. Unfortunately, these are mainly located in Java, where the possibilities of hydro-electric power are far less than in Sumatra. Nevertheless, a government project at Tjitarum in West Java will eventually be of considerable assistance.

Until the mid nineteen-thirties industrial activity in Indonesia was concerned with the factory processing of agricultural and mineral goods for export, and with cottage industry for the domestic market. The production of consumer goods did not begin until 1935, when the world market for many Indonesian products went into decline.

Now one may distinguish three divisions within industry: the first consists of cottage industry, labour rather than capital-intensive, employing less than ten full-time workers and no mechanization. The second is of medium-scale industry, employing between ten and fifty full-time workers and between one and five installed horse-power. Large-scale or factory industry is anything bigger.

Cottage industry is the only form which uses labour intensively and offers the only real hope of providing work for Indonesia's many millions. It is the largest employer outside agriculture, providing work for several times more people than factory industry, among them women or agricultural labourers seasonally unemployed. Its products include silverware, batik and hand-woven cloths, and Indonesian cigarettes. Simple equipment is used, and usually made locally. This industry fits very well into the social structure, being organized on the basis of close personal relationships between owners and labourers. However, it does not encourage modern industrial habits, but permits a high rate of absenteeism, sporadic employment, and no discipline. It supports the traditional social structure; it does not work to change it.

Also producing consumer goods are the medium-sized industries. There has been a rapid growth in this field since 1950, and though it does not promise to provide much employment it nevertheless offers the greatest hope for producing Indonesian entrepreneurs. Short of capital and with inadequate transport facilities, both the size of the unit and the market tend to be limited.

These industries are modern in character. Their business is specialized and constant, the entrepreneur is the principal agent, and costs are more carefully calculated. However, unlike the large factories, they are small enough to permit the persistence of friendly relations between managers and workers; they are therefore relatively free from labour troubles.

The large-sized factories are mostly those which have relatively high capital investment per worker and of course use power. Their usual function is to process estate produce for the world market; some large factories, however, turn out consumer goods to satisfy the internal demand.

Indonesia invests only about 5 per cent of its national income, which is barely enough to provide for its growing population, leave alone any increase in production. Naturally, a poor country like Indonesia cannot save much. But there does appear to be a fair amount of loose cash lying idle, mainly due to the lack of entre-preneurs to put it to profitable use. In addition, much of the aid given Indonesia, as well as money raised by taxation, has not been used as productively as it might have been.

Foreign Aid

In addition to her own resources, Indonesia has received capital from abroad. Even before sovereignty was transferred in 1949, Marshall Plan assistance began to come into the country. Since then aid has come in a thickening stream, especially after Indonesia began to pursue an 'independent and active' foreign policy and was able to obtain help from all sides in the world struggle. Table I indicates the source, amounts, and type of aid given.

TABLE I

FOREIGN AID TO INDONESIA 1950–1961/2
$ million

Donor	Grants	Sales of Foodstuffs*	Loans	Credits	Arms	Total
United States	70·3	304·6	205·4	—	?	580·3
Other Western countries	20·8	—	226·4	55·0	—	302·2
Japan	177·0	—	100·0	—	—	277·0
USSR and East Europe	—	—	593·7	—	1000·0	1593·7
China	—	—	50·0	15·0	—	65·0
Yugoslavia	—	—	25·0	—	—	25·0
United Nations	9·6	—	—	—	—	9·6
	277·7	304·6	1200·5	70·0	1000·0	2852·8

* Food sold by the US government against payment in rupiah which are retained in Indonesia for use on development projects.

One may add that aid from Japan has been by way of reparations, and that she has also promised to provide further grants of $223 million and loans of $100 million over a twelve-year period. Indonesia has also signed agreements for technical assistance and co-operation with the Soviet Union and East European countries by which they send specialists to Indonesia, and Indonesians are sent to Europe for training. By July 1961 some 300 technicians from communist countries were working in Indonesia, and about 300 Indonesian students were receiving training in those countries.

Under American technical assistance there were in 1961 some 200 specialists in the country, principally in education, transportation, public health and sanitation, agriculture and fisheries, and public administration. Up to July of that year approximately 4,410 Indonesians had received or were receiving specialized training financed by aid in Western countries, and about 1,200 Indonesians were being trained in those countries every year.

Soviet loans have helped to construct an iron and steel mill, a fertilizer plant, 662 kilometres of new roads, and two mechanized rice enterprises in Borneo, to provide technical assistance in prospecting for sulphur and phosphates, and to investigate the peaceful uses of atomic energy, to launch a faculty of Oceanography at Amboina in the Moluccas, a non-ferrous metal industry, a chemical industry, textile factories, agricultural projects, and rehabilitation of the tin-mines on Bangka Island. Some $12·5 million were used to build the Asian Games complex of stadia, etc., in Djakarta.

The loans from the United States have been used for various projects, including transport, power and telecommunications, a large cement factory, the purchase of aircraft, a thermal station, repairs to ports and harbours and to the railway in South Sumatra, an assembly unit for jeeps, diesel generators, and repairs to and construction of roads.

By supplying surplus agricultural commodities to Indonesia for rupiah payment, the United States provides food (rice and wheat flour), cotton, and tobacco without being paid in convertible currency. Up to 1962 some $304·6 million were received in sales; of this amount, $224 million were made available to Indonesia as grants and loans for mutually agreed projects, such as a major irrigation project in West Java, road rehabilitation, and an agricultural experimental station.

The total amount of aid or offers of aid Indonesia has received from 1956 to the end of 1962 has been estimated at $2,700 million. This means that Indonesia has been signing aid agreements at the

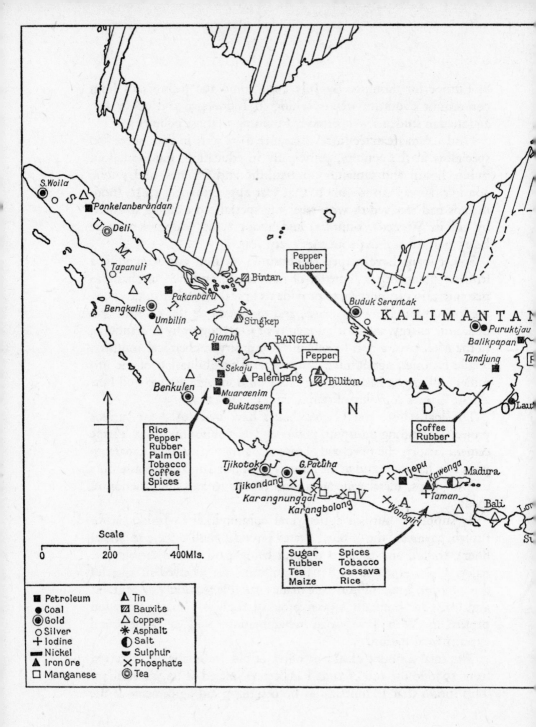

S. Woila
Pankelanberandan
Deli
Tapanuli
Pakanbaru
Bengkalis
Umbilin
Djambi
Sekaju
Benkulen
Muaraenim
Bukitasem

U M A T R A

Bintan
Singkep

BANGKA
Palembang
Billiton

I   N   D

Pepper
Rubber

Buduk Serantak

K A L I M A N T A N
Puruktjau
Balikpapan
Tandjung

Pepper

Coffee
Rubber

Laut

Rice
Pepper
Rubber
Palm Oil
Tobacco
Coffee
Spices

Tjikotok
Tjikondang
Karangnunggal
Karangbolong

G. Patuha
V
Wongiri
A

Tjepu
Kawenga
Taman
Madura

Bali
Lor
St

Scale

0   200   400 Mls.

Sugar   Spices
Rubber   Tobacco
Tea   Cassava
Maize   Rice

■ Petroleum   ▲ Tin
● Coal   ▨ Bauxite
◉ Gold   △ Copper
○ Silver   ✳ Asphalt
✛ Iodine   ◐ Salt
▬ Nickel   ◡ Sulphur
▲ Iron Ore   ✕ Phosphate
□ Manganese   ◎ Tea

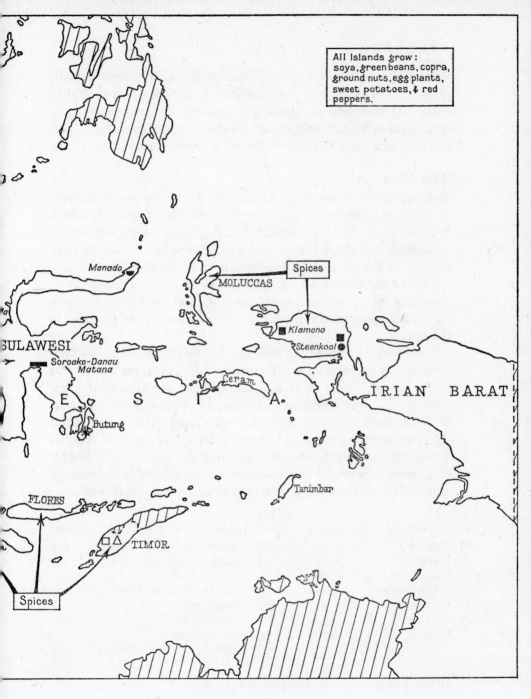

All Islands grow:
soya, green beans, copra,
ground nuts, egg plants,
sweet potatoes, & red
peppers.

Spices

Manado

MOLUCCAS

SULAWESI

Klamono

Steenkool

Soroako-Danau
Matana

Ceram

IRIAN BARAT

E S I A

Butung

Tanimbar

FLORES

TIMOR

Spices

Economic map of Indonesia

annual rate of about $400 million, while she has been actually receiving something like $200 million per annum. This should be compared with total government expenditure for 1960 of the then equivalent of $1,022 million and exports worth $840 million. This situation was likely to continue for the next few years.

The Plan

Indonesia's first serious plan for economic development emerged only in 1960. It is the Eight-Year Development Plan (1961–9), which has two parts. Part A consists of 374 projects which are directly concerned with development, and which are to be financed by eight projects in Part B, mainly in agriculture and mining.

For the first three years the plan emphasizes growing more food, especially rice, producing more clothing, and improving distribution. Subsequently, the heavier industrial projects are to come to the fore.

However, the continuing inflation has meant that little has been done to implement the plan. Its major achievement, perhaps, is that it has brought home to at least some in the government that the success of the Part B projects and therefore of the whole plan depends on Indonesia's ability to attract foreign capital. This has modified the government's traditional hostility to foreign investment, and has brought it to evolve the idea of 'production sharing', whereby foreign investment is regarded as a redeemable loan, repayable in shares of output. The distribution of Part A projects by category is as follows:

CATEGORY	Rp. '000 mn.	Per cent of total	CATEGORY	Rp. '000 mn.	Per cent of total
Cultural	1·6	0·6	Industry	52·0	21·7
Educational	16·3	6·8	Health	2·2	0·9
Research	2·6	1·1	Transport and		
Public Welfare	6·2	2·6	Communications	60·2	25·1
Government	3·6	1·5	Finance and		
Food	25·1	10·5	Tourism	11·3	4·7
Clothing	28·9	12·0	Special Project		
			(Military)	30·0	12·5
	84·3	35·1		155·7	64·9

TOTAL EXPENDITURE: RP. 240,000 MILLION

Of this total expenditure, Rp. 133,000 million are to be spent in Indonesian currency, Rp. 77,000 million in foreign exchange. The foreign exchange component of the Special Project for the Military is not known. The following table shows the expected receipts from the Part B projects:

Rp. '000 mn.

	Foreign Exchange revenue*	Rupiah revenue
Oil: government share of exports	53·1	—
Foreign companies' capital converted into rupiah	33·7	—
Timber: export increase	2·4	—
Fish: savings on imports	0·6	—
Copra: export increase	3·4	—
Rubber: export increase	14·4	—
Tin: export increase	0·7	—
Aluminium: export increase	0·5	—
Tourism	2·0	—
Proceeds of 1959 monetary reform	—	10
Share of State enterprise profits	—	32
Community saving	—	8
Sales of shares and bonds	—	8
Sale of capital goods	—	16
Sale of consumer goods	—	46
* At rate prevalent at the time ($1=Rp. 45).	110·8	120

These projects are therefore supposed to produce nearly Rp. 120,000 million in domestic currency and nearly $2,500 million in foreign exchange (the Part A projects are assumed to require $2,200 million). Over $1,900 million of this amount is expected from the export of oil and the portion of new oil company investment spent in Indonesia. Unfortunately, no estimate has been made of expenses, so the net revenue is not known. The United States Economic Aid Team to Indonesia[7] estimated that only on the most optimistic assumption would the net foreign yield exceed the estimate; taking a pessimistic view, the net revenue would fall short of requirements by over $1,100 million.

The Plan placed emphasis on consumption in the early years, and had no provision for any increase in taxation. This was clearly motivated by the government's fear of unpopularity. It is no great exaggeration to say that foreign investors, especially the oil companies, were expected to pay for Indonesia's development.

Nor can the calculations in the Plan itself be absolved from criticism. While an attempt was made to assess the capital costs of the various projects, no estimate was made of their future operating and maintenance cost, nor of the alternative uses to which the same resources might be put, nor of methods of accomplishing the same objectives with fewer resources.

The Plan seemed unduly hopeful, and experience since its inception has done nothing to support its optimism. It assumed, for instance, that rice production would increase by about 9 per cent a year; in fact, the usual increases before and after the inception of the Plan were more of the order of 2 to 4 per cent, while the 1963 crop suffered from a plague of mice.

Food

Indonesia's economic activities must be measured against the yardstick of her population. This was 60 million in 1930; by 1961 it has risen to 97 million, or by nearly 62 per cent. This is a simple rate of growth of 2 per cent per annum. Those responsible for the 1961 census estimated that during the ten preceding years the population had grown by 2·2 per cent per annum.

The first material requirement for any country is, of course, food, and self-sufficiency in rice has been an oft-repeated aim of Indonesian governments. But between 1940 and 1960 total food production had risen only 22·5 per cent. Table II shows the production trends for rice, maize, and cassava, the three most important food crops, from 1951 to 1961 and 1962. Rice has risen 52 per cent between 1951 and 1962. Cassava and maize, inferior as foods, had increased by 70 per cent in a decade.

TABLE II

PRINCIPAL FARM FOOD CROPS 1951–62
'000 metric tons

Year	Rice (paddy)	Maize	Cassava
1951	11,969	1,398	7,134
1954	15,061	2,720	9,569
1957	14,677	1,860	10,118
1960	16,423	2,486	11,142
1961	16,000	2,380	12,100
1962	18,200	—	—

The government has a system of buying rice from the peasantry and selling it to areas of rice shortage and to government and Army personnel at subsidized rates. But the price offered is only a small fraction of the free market rate, and the peasants are naturally un-willing either to increase production or to sell to the government. Not surprisingly, government procurement policy has failed completely, and it was estimated that for 1963 some 1·3 million tons would have to be imported, at a cost of about $130 million (£46·5 million). This subsidized sale artificially inflates the demand for rice, and is estimated to cost the government some Rp. 5,000 million a year, quite apart from the cost of rice imports.

According to the United States Economic Aid Team[8] even the aim of self-sufficiency in rice was questionable. They believed that agricultural resources would be better used if corn and tapioca were to continue to serve as substitutes for rice, as in the past, with corn being exported to exchange for rice. This required that the goal be self-sufficiency in foodstuffs as a whole rather than in rice alone.

The Team recommended that higher prices be offered to the producers. So far, however, the government has not heeded this advice. Nor is it difficult to understand why. If it did pay the peasant higher prices, but continued to provide rice below cost to the privileged categories, there would be greater pressure to include more people among the privileged, and inflation would be accelerated.

Cash Crops

The performance of cash crops is reflected in Table III. If anything, they have done worse than other products of Indonesian agriculture. Sugar, tea, palm-oil, copra, tobacco, were all below 1938 levels, and also below 1957 levels. Rubber and coffee, while they were above 1938 levels, were below those of 1957, a natural consequence of the expulsion of trained Dutch estate managers.

TABLE III

PRODUCTION OF MAJOR CASH CROPS
'000 metric tons, unless otherwise shown

Year	Rubber	Sugar	Tea mn. lb.	Palm-oil	Copra	Tobacco	Coffee
1938	321	1,400	176	227	354	49·2	46
1957	696	828	103·5	160	312	14·55	75
1959	705	856	96·5	138	176	15·48	90
1961	681	627	94·6	146	273	16·97	90
1962	670	592	101·8	—	—	—	—

For a long time, until 1959, Indonesia was the world's largest producer of natural rubber, contributing between 35 and 45 per cent of world natural production and approximately 20 to 30 per cent of total (natural and synthetic) production. After 1959 Malaya, having developed and planted new high-yielding trees, took over that position.

Between 1952 and 1959 the output of dry rubber from small-holdings remained relatively constant at about 310 lb. per acre. The average yield from the estates, however, declined from 675 to 450 lb. per acre. Several factors accounted for this, most of which can be laid at the door of unstable government. Smallholders, on the other hand, increased their production; they drained their existing trees and planted others of, unfortunately, a low-yielding variety.

The economically productive life of the rubber tree averages only thirty-five years, and about one-third of the rubber estates is in trees over this age, while another third is over twenty-six years old. The smallholders' position is worse: 50 to 60 per cent of their plantings is no longer productive. Of the areas replanted, immature areas which will come into production in the next few years are less than 12 per cent of the estates' and 3 per cent of the smallholders' areas. In 1963 production was estimated to have fallen to 580,000 metric tons, and it seems that nothing can prevent a further decline during the next several years.

Table III also shows that in the past five years sugar production has declined by a quarter, and in 1962 was below half the 1938 figure. Sugar factories numbered 170 in 1938; there were only 54 in 1962, and their equipment was obsolete or run-down. They offer such poor prices that the planted acreage has fallen from 64,000 acres in 1955 to 25,000 in 1962. This decline comes at a particularly unfortunate time, as it appears that there will be a world shortage of sugar for at least the near future, and in any case there will be a long-term growth of demand within Indonesia.

With regard to tea, an attack of a leaf disease known as 'blister blight', and the political vicissitudes suffered by the estates, have prevented their rehabilitation; the smallholders were ruined by the same disease. Not surprisingly, tea is now a relatively depressed feature of the economy.

Copra occupies an important place in Indonesia's development plans, as it was expected to produce some $76 million (£27 million) in foreign exchange revenue, forming 3·1 per cent of total expected receipts from the Part B projects. However, as in the case of rubber, most of the trees are over-aged, making any increase in output dependent on new planting. This does not appear to be happening, and copra production is also likely to continue to decline in the near future at least. Only between 20 and 25 per cent of copra is exported, while a considerable amount is lost owing to inadequate transport and distribution and much smuggling.

Tobacco and palm-oil estates have been in the same political boat as the rubber plantations; their production record tells its own tale.

Minerals

With the passage of the years, ever less coal has been mined; as Table IV indicates, the decline has not been interrupted since 1939 except briefly in 1954. Of greater importance for foreign exchange is tin, which is produced almost entirely for export. The world price of tin rose sharply in 1962, but with the mines long neglected, Indonesia was unable to profit from this development. After another sharp rise in 1963 the world tin market was stabilized at about £900 a ton, but the Indonesian tin industry was in no position to benefit. For to rehabilitate the mines requires foreign investment of the order of $75 million (£27 million), and Indonesia's xenophobia has frightened away foreign investors. Bauxite presents a somewhat more hopeful picture, as its current production is above that of 1939; however, it is also considerably below that of 1951. Exceptionally, the production of petroleum continues to increase. The reason is that it is controlled not by the Indonesian government, but by the international oil companies.

TABLE IV

MINERAL PRODUCTION

'000 metric tons

Year	Coal	Tin (concentrates)	Bauxite (crude ore)	Petroleum
1939	1,781	28·3	231	7,949
1951	868	31·5	642	8,093
1954	900	36·4	173	10,775
1957	717	28·2	241	15,468
1960	657	23·0	396	20,800
1962	472	17·6	—	22,788
1963	—	12·8	—	—

With production falling in virtually every sphere, and with population constantly increasing, the Indonesian's standard of living necessarily continued to decline. The *per capita* domestic product was lower in 1959 than it had been in 1955. The Indonesian has been in a situation of continuous impoverishment for several decades; his state seems to be worsening rapidly. The Indonesian government has shown no genuine desire, leave alone ability, to halt the downward trend. The budget for 1961, for example, revealed that only 35 per cent of expenditure was being placed in development activities, defined generously. Some 40 per cent of the budget went into 'defence' alone.

With little growth in production to increase the tax harvest, revenues have been far below expenditure, as Table V reveals:

TABLE V

GOVERNMENT REVENUE AND EXPENDITURE
Rp. million

	1957	1958	1959	1960	1961	1962	1963
Revenue	16,873	19,656	30,346	50,318	62,759	77,205	272,024
Expend.	22,173	31,696	44,350	58,336	79,624	116,809	305,618
Balance	—5,300	—12,040	—14,004	—8,018	—16,865	—39,604	—33,594

MONEY SUPPLY AND CREDIT AT END OF YEAR
Rp. million

	1958	1959	1960	1961	1962	Relative growth
Currency outside banks	19,870	26,390	34,080	48,750	102,280	1
Total money supply	29,370	34,890	47,840	67,860	135,330	4
Advance to government	29,880	33,680	34,450	60,730	121,370	3
Advances to private sector	6,560	13,080	19,890	29,150	36,380	2

The gap between revenue and expenditure has been bridged by the simple expedient of printing more currency notes and granting more credit. The consequences on prices have been predictably disastrous. The Central Bureau of Statistics compiles an index of the prices of nineteen foodstuffs on the free market in Djakarta, taking 1953 as the base year (=100). By the first quarter of 1962 it had climbed to 1,287; by the first quarter of the next year it was 2,515, while the latest figure in this series, that for December 1963, is 4,674.[9] With increasing military expenditure as a result of hostilities against Malaysia, there was every prospect of the index continuing to soar. One result, of course, has been successive devaluations of the rupiah, the latest in 1964, when the official rate of $1=Rp. 45 was made meaningless by the adoption of rates between $1:Rp. 250 and $1:Rp. 2,250, depending on the item to be imported, with the 'conversion rate' set at $1:Rp. 315.[10]

What has bedevilled the Indonesian economy has been the light-hearted attitude of senior officials towards the inflation, which has swollen the demand for imports, made consumption more profitable than exports and hoarding more than production, so that resources have been diverted to the wrong uses. The Indonesian government has attempted to deal with the problem by direct controls. This has simply wasted the talents of some of its best administrators, has siphoned foreign exchange to the black market and away from government, and has increased the incentives for corruption.

Not only has the Indonesian standard of living not been raised, but the economy has become no stronger. Nearly 80 per cent of Indonesia's foreign exchange is produced by exports of two commodities, rubber and tin; the country is therefore more, not less, vulnerable than was the case before the war. And the proportion of the national product represented by manufacturing, which was 10 per cent before the war, has now declined to only 8 per cent. Immediately before the Second World War, there were some 300,000 Indonesians working in factories; in 1960 the number was estimated at 427,000; which represents a smaller proportion of the population. Economically, Indonesia is declining rather than developing, and it is difficult to argue that aid has been productive.

64 Four out of five Indonesians are on the land. The size of hol[d]ing only permits subsistence farming and many families have to [do] anything, such as keeping live stock seen here at Bali, to supple ment their incomes.

65 All aspects of life are governed by belief in a number of supernatural forces. This burial figure is typical of the Batak people of Sumatra.

66 President Sukarno launched the abortive Eight-Year Development Plan in 1961. It emphasized partly the growing of more food, the production of more clothing and the improvement of distribution.

67 (*left*) Rubber is one of Indonesia's most important exports. A family in Sumatra prepare crude sheets of congealed rubber.

68 Copra, the dried meat of the coconut, is the next most important agricultural export and can be grown anywhere in the archipelago. This is at Surabaya in Java.

69 (*left*) Maize, a subsidiary food crop, is grown mainly in the *tegalan* (dry fields) of Java. This is an experimental maize-growing station.

70 (*right*) Although the mining of coal is now on the decline it has been an important industry. A mine at Samarinda in East Borneo.

71, 72 (*below*) Cottage industry is the largest employer outside agriculture. Its products include silverware (*left*) and Batik cloth (*right*).

73 A traditional Balinese painting illustrates the characteristic quality of this art-form.

74 Balinese dancing is more lively than that of Java and has long been part of Bali's culture. These two girls are performing a dance called the *legong*.

75 The performance of the *wayang kulit* (shadow play) has a predominantly religious and magical significance.

76 Woodcarving is an art which still flourishes in Indonesia.

77 The *gamelan* percussion orchestra accompanies the performance of the *wayang kulit*. This is at Peliatan in Bali.

11   Contemporary Arts

Background

IN THE CREATION OF A NATION, forms of artistic expression have a part to play perhaps as important as that of social, economic, and political factors. It is not surprising, therefore, that with the development of national consciousness in the years after 1920, a discussion began on the form that Indonesian art should take. Two points of view were opposed:

1 that a national culture should grow out of the higher forms of the local cultures: it would be only a new development of the past;
2 that a national culture should be new, disregarding local cultures, while the traditional elements would have to be regarded as products of local culture on a lower level.

This debate, like so many others, reflected the opposition between the Javanese and the other peoples of Indonesia. As their culture is the most evolved, the Javanese champion the first point of view, since superior forms of their arts will certainly be the most important. The spokesmen of the other peoples tend to take the other standpoint, and demand that all cultures should be treated equally, relegated to the past, and a new culture created which would favour none of the local ones. With the achievement of political hegemony by the Javanese, the first point of view has been officially followed.

The contemporary arts in Indonesia fall into two broad categories: the Western-influenced and the traditional. Western-influenced arts put an emphasis on wholes, following their European nineteenth-century inspiration; their content is realistic; the artists are known as individuals; and they try to achieve an Indonesian culture, as distinct from a purely local one. Traditional art, on the other hand, puts emphasis on detail; its symbolic roots lie in traditional beliefs; its content is predominantly idealized; its practitioner is anonymous; and it is rooted in the local cultures of the various ethnic groups.

For example, traditional Balinese paintings elaborate the details of every part of a scene; modern artists allow their colours to convey a general impression. *Wayang* stories tell about stylized personalities in ideal circumstances; a modern novelist will depict living characters in real situations. Traditional Indonesian art was collective; modern Indonesian art and literature are individual products.

Some of Indonesia's artistic traditions go back to prehistoric times; others to the Indian period (*c.* 200–1500); yet others to the Islamic period (*c.* 1500–1800); the Moluccas, exceptionally, were strongly influenced by Portuguese culture; the modern school owes its origins to the Dutch period (*c.* 1800–1942); whilst a not inconsiderable stimulus was imparted during the Japanese occupation (1942–5).

One useful effect of the occupation was to convince the Indonesian cultural public that European artists were not necessarily superior to their own. In consequence, they devoted much more attention not only to their traditional art, but also to those Indonesians who worked in a Western medium. The momentum thus acquired was not lost in the period of struggle against the Dutch, when culture acquired a propaganda value, nor in independent Indonesia, when it was deliberately fostered. The most important forms of Indonesian cultural expression are perhaps literature, music, dance, and drama, the plastic and graphic arts, and ornamentation. It may be of interest to consider them in that order.

Literature

Though all ethnic groups in Indonesia have a traditional style of verbal expression, only the Malay and Javanese groups have an important literary history of many centuries. The Javanese literary tradition goes back to the ninth century at least, the Malay to the sixteenth. Written literary activity was carried on in court and religious centres; in Javanese in Central and East Java and Bali; and in Malay in Sumatra and the coastal areas of Borneo and the Celebes.

The simplest and most general forms of verbal expression in the archipelago are the two- and four-line verses such as are used for the *pantun* of the Malays and similar forms of poetry among the other ethnic groups. These forms may be much elaborated, resulting in some very complex patterns. They may be love-songs, war-songs, magic spells used by shamans, and prayers by priests.

Nearly all the forms of verbal expression of the various ethnic groups in Indonesia feature figures of heroes, divine tricksters, jokers, and animals of the Indian epics. There is a certain basic similarity in all these forms. The heroes are usually associated with divine beings or ancestor-figures, and sometimes genealogically connected with the gods. The hero's birth is often supernatural; he may be the result of sexual intercourse between a god and a woman on earth; or he may be found as a baby in a furrow in the rice-fields and brought up by an ordinary peasant. The divine trickster acts as an intermediary between the profane and sacred worlds; he is both god and human being; male and female; a stupid clown and the acme of wisdom. Central to all these stories is the idea of the stupid or the small man, who is cleverer than the wise or the mighty. For instance, many ethnic groups have stories about the *kantjil* (mouse-deer), represented as a smart little animal able to fool bigger and stronger animals.

There are hundreds of written manuscripts enshrining the Javanese literary tradition. The language used, now known as *Djawa Kuno* (ancient Javanese), was probably never employed in ordinary speech. It was much influenced by Sanskrit. The Javanese court poets used Sanskrit verse techniques, while the products of court literature were versions in prose and poetry of the Hindu epics *Mahabharata* and *Ramayana*, or of Hindu religious handbooks.

In the latter part of the Madjapahit period (from 1400 to 1500), Sanskrit influence gave way to Javanese, while in the later Islamic period this material was accumulated and mixed with Islamic elements into historical mythological handbooks. These are in verse

167

form, and are still recited in many families. In addition, Islamic brotherhoods, which were widespread over Java, developed a type of religious literature, telling of Muslim saints who were former religious teachers in Java.

Literary work in Malay from about 1500 was concentrated in the court centres of Malaya and North Sumatra; its main sources were in the Islamic literature from Persia and Arabia. Like Javanese Islamic literature, it developed an historical-mythological court tradition; while in Atjeh Islamic mystical poetry emerged.

Javanese and Malay literature died almost completely in the eigh-teenth and nineteenth centuries. However, the writings of Abdullah ibn Abdulkadir, Raffles's translator, set a new trend by deviating from the traditional Malay literary forms. His autobiography, and one of his best-known prose works, the *Hikayat Abdullah*, was perhaps the earliest example of works influenced by contact with the West.[11]

The Western style only gained popularity, however, during the development of nationalism. This in turn led to a demand for a national language; and since Malay was already the lingua franca of the archipelago, a variant, Indonesian, was evolved to meet the need. It became the basis of the development of modern Indonesian litera-ture. A new school of writing was created by a group of authors calling themselves Pudjangga Baru (New Authors); among the most important of its members was Takdir Alisjahbana. This group consisted mostly of people from Sumatra, who held the second point of view on development of Indonesian culture mentioned above, namely that it should disregard local cultures and the past. This school was important both in the development of Indonesian litera-ture and in the development of modern Indonesian as a language. It looked to the West for its inspiration. Another group of writers, however, who were Islamic in sentiment and inclination, looked rather towards Egypt.

The next most important school, in order of time, was the Angkatan 45 (Group of 1945), composed of a number of new authors who, during the Japanese occupation, when Indonesian became the official language, had studied the work of foreign authors such as André Gide, Ernest Hemingway, and the Dutch writer

Menno ter Braak. Their leading member, Chairil Anwar, unfortunately died at the very early age of twenty-seven. They emphasized
the link between the artist and society. However, with the growth of
totalitarian tendencies in Indonesia, many of these voices have been
stilled. Prominent among them one may mention Mochtar Lubis,
whose book *Twilight in Djakarta* has been translated and published
abroad whilst he languishes in jail.[12]

Music, Dance and Drama

These arts are important for many of the Indonesian ethnic groups,
and they are often intimately related one to the other. They have
remained almost completely traditional in form and content. We
know very little about their history; it does appear, however, that
the Javanese courts of the Indian period had an elaborate art of
dancing and music, which survived in the Muslim period despite
the disapproval of such activities by Islamic religious law.

The forms of music vary greatly. Some groups in Sumatra feature
drums in Islamic music; other regions in the same island emphasize
flutes or stringed instruments; Java and Bali emphasize percussion
instruments; areas in East Indonesia, such as Amboina, have more
rhythmical songs with string accompaniment, very similar to
Hawaiian music.

Today the *krontjong*, a romantic type of stringed music, attempts to
achieve the status of a national Indonesian musical style. It appears
to have been originally introduced in the sixteenth century by the
Portuguese. Subsequently adapted by the Eurasians, it practically became their 'folk music'. Later, however, it was taken up by the poor
in the urban slums. After the war it underwent an improvement and
is now probably the most widespread form of music in Indonesia.

The Javanese *gamelan* orchestra merits specific attention. It is
composed exclusively of percussion instruments (*gamel* means
hammer in Javanese). The five-tone scale sounds odd to the
Westerner, as the intervals are unusual. Also, there are no modula-
tions, and melodies are not based on a fixed keynote.

Gamelan music is essentially auxiliary, whether to Javanese
dancing, or festivals, or processions, or other special occasions. It is

polyphonic; some instruments play the basic theme, others the ornamental variations and counter-melodies, whilst others keep time, and a fourth group regulates the musical paraphrasing and inter-punctuations. Its polyphony, however, is much freer than that of Western music. The orchestra consists of a number of instruments (gongs, drums, *sarons*, the *rehab*, the *gender*, and the *gambang*), male and female soloists, and a chorus which always sings in unison. All the singing is nasal and the singers turn their heads away from the audience.

The main function of the gongs is to act as paraphrasing instru-ments. They come in various sizes and nearly all of them have a magnificent long-echoing note. The drums consist of conical or full-bellied resonating chambers, with skins stretched across the two open sides, and resting upon cross-beams. They are beaten with both hands. Their task, especially the large drum, is to mark the tempo. The sarons (convex metal resonating keys, beaten with small mallets) and the rebab (a two-stringed instrument, played like a 'cello) play the basic theme. The gender is composed of small bronze slabs suspended freely by two cords in a row. Under each slab there is a resonating tube, tuned to the same pitch, which gives the tone the necessary resonance. The instrument is played with two small round sticks, and as soon as a slab is struck, it is damped by the same hand. The function of this instrument is to develop the nuclear theme, and accompany the *dalang* (see below) as he sings. The gambang, a trough xylophone, with wooden keys which are also struck with round sticks, has a soft and full tone, and performs much the same function as the gender.

These instruments form the typical gamelan orchestra. For special occasions others may be included, such as the only wind instrument in the orchestra, the *suling*, a type of flute.

The best and most popular gamelan orchestras are to be found in the courts of the principalities in Central Java. At the court of Jogyakarta there is a very ancient one, traditionally believed to have been founded in the Kingdom of Madjapahit, which is allowed to play only in the week devoted to commemorating the birth and death of the Prophet Muhammad. This was the only type of gamelan which Islam tolerated, and then only to facilitate conversion. However, once having done so, it could not control the evolution of the gamelan. New compositions, instrumental and vocal, were created. These were typically collective efforts; the individual composer is unknown to the gamelan orchestra.

In any discussion of Indonesian drama, the Javanese and Balinese shadow play, the *wayang kulit* (literally, shadow of leather) requires special mention. Performed with flat leather puppets, it was already both popular and generally known by the year 1000, and was subsequently strongly influenced by Indian culture. It survived the collapse of Madjapahit, withstood Islam, and was used by the nationalists to spread their message during the struggle against the Dutch. It is still the most popular entertainment in Java.

The wayang performance has always had a magic and religious significance. The puppets, and also the moving silhouettes, suggested ancestors; the interpreter of this mysterious event was considered as the priest who established contact between the living and the dead. The wayang kulit has retained this magic character; even in the present day it may be performed to avert some disaster.

The properties required are very few. They consist of a transparent white cloth stretched on a vertical wooden frame; a lamp, the light from which falls on the white cloth, the leather puppets, and a dalang to manipulate them, ensuring that their show falls on the screen. A great number of puppets appear in the performance, since each one represents a different character. Behind the dalang there is the gamelan orchestra, to which he gives cues by tapping a small hammer of horn or hardwood.

Customarily, when the wayang performance takes place indoors, the men sit next to the dalang, while the women sit behind the screen, and thus see only the shadows of the figures. When it is performed in the open air, both men and women sit on the side of the screen opposite the dalang.

The dalang is the key-man, who only attains his position after several years' training. He not only moves the puppets, but also speaks the various parts, and in between acts as a narrator. He must ensure that the performance lasts from half past seven in the evening until six o'clock the next morning. During the performance he must not move from the screen, and may not say anything other than that which is part of the 'script'. He must modulate his voice to suit each of the characters portrayed, and must be familiar with the forms of speech they use. He must of course know exactly with which puppet any character may be represented. In one play alone he may have to portray thirty-seven main characters, each of which will play many parts. Most of the wayang plays have not been completely scripted. The dalang only has a brief summary of the play, on which he can construct his improvisations, though the range of these is fairly limited.

The gamelan orchestra opens the performance with a long intro-duction, after which the dalang describes the kraton in which the action takes place and the characters in the play. The performance itself begins at nine o'clock in the evening. It falls into three parts: the introduction, the actual plot, and the denouement, with the triumph of good over evil. Each of these three parts takes three hours to recite. However, even when the subject-matter is identical, each performance differs from every other.

The wayang puppets are flat, coloured pieces of parchment, and always highly stylized, both with regard to the reproduction of the human figure and the grooming, clothes, and jewellery. Of course, the figures are symbolical rather than realistic. The colours need not be natural; the skin is mostly gilded or black, while the face may be painted in various colours. Originally, these figures were much more naturalistic, but Islamic disapproval of the portrayal of the human figure forced their present stylization.

The face and feet are always in profile, while the body is turned partly to the front. The legs are held either wide apart or close together. Warriors and rough characters have theirs wide apart; female figures close together. Many modifications are possible in the shape of the head, the expression of the face, leg posture, and colour-ing of the decorations. Each figure can be shaped individually, and its size can be adjusted to suggest the character symbolized.

The face of the puppets is also stylized to suggest character. Fore-head and nose form one straight line to suggest a noble disposition;

the nose is delicately shaped; the eyes are slit. Demonic types have round eyes and large, often crudely shaped noses, set at an angle to the line of the forehead, and a threatening expression. Equally, the size of the figures has a symbolic meaning: demons (giants), gods, human beings, and so on, all vary in size.

The tales which are portrayed by the wayang kulit, known as *lakons*, are a mixture of indigenous and alien elements. The art itself is entirely native, and originally may well have depicted the exploits of heroic ancestors from mythical antiquity. But with the incursion of Indian cultural influence, Javanese adaptations of Indian myths and sagas appeared. The religious worship of ancestors was not displaced, but rather the events described in the Indian tales were transplanted to a Javanese environment, with the context being set by traditional Javanese ideas. Thus, in the long run, the old sacred myths were combined with the new tales; deified ancestors were identified with Indian gods and heroes, or were allotted their place in the lakon in a new form that was hardly recognizable.

Three groups of characters are to be found in the lakons: gods, demons (giants), and men. Basically, all these stories portray the struggle between good and evil. The gods in the lakons are often unable to resist the attacks of the demons. It is always a man, possessing extraordinary magic and great courage, who comes to their help, and succeeds in turning the scales in their favour. Apart from one group of lakons which deal with early history, the others all incorporate figures from Hindu mythology together with purely Javanese characters. The epic richest in source-material for the wayang plays has been the *Mahabharata*, but the setting has been transposed from ancient India to Java, and it is the Javanese who live to experience the final triumph of good over evil.

Every wayang performance features three characters which are of some interest: Semar and his two sons, Petruk and Nalagareng. All three appear as rustic buffoons, but Semar in addition is the servant of the hero of the moment, and thus frequently his adviser, often more perceptive than his master. At times he even controls magic forces and can encompass the ruin of mighty demons. He thrusts his way forward to the very seat of the gods; and sometimes incarnates a deity. The names of all three do not come from Indian literature, but are old Javanese. These characters are probably a survival of the ancient ancestor cult.

There are several other types of wayang, of which the most important are the *wayang golek*, the *wayang topeng*, and the *wayang wong*.

In the wayang golek the puppets are three-dimensional and made of wood, and may be operated by the dalang in such a fashion that the puppet gives the impression of being alive. This play is performed both by day and by night. The story is closely connected with the penetration of Islam into Java. The puppets are similar to those of the wayang kulit, but are not so highly stylized. In consequence, there is greater variation in their artistic value, though the best examples display designs with very human features.

In both the wayang topeng and the wayang wong the puppets are replaced by human performers. In the wayang topeng the actors are masked, and do not speak; the dalang acts as in the wayang kulit. In the wayang wong, the actors are not masked and speak, while the dalang plays a lesser role. Both types of wayang include dances. Those of the wayang topeng, with the dancers masked, derive from the primitive masked dances of Java, though they have been influenced by Hinduism. The ceremonial, and frequently, magic, character survived.

The wayang wong evolved during the later nineteenth century, and the style of its dances is similar to that of the wayang topeng. But whilst no group dances occur in the wayang topeng, they are usual in the wayang wong, and are accompanied by the gamelan. The groups are either of men or of women, female parts being sometimes performed by men.

The Balinese counterpart of the wayang topeng and wayang wong is the open-air play: also with gamelan accompaniment. It is performed in the court of a temple; and the main characters are fiendish, expressing the feeling of the Balinese that they are continually threatened by demonic forces. The figures are grotesque, and the actors, who all wear masks, are able to convey their emotions through gestures. These plays are so realistic that they inspire terror in the audience.

The open-air play is not truly a wayang play, as it does not derive its plots from the Indian epics. The Balinese do, however, have such plays, in which the masks worn portray characters from these narratives. There are many actors, and each has a mask with facial expressions adapted to every appearance. The masks themselves display a cultural difference from the Javanese. The latter are both more refined and more detached; the Balinese masks represent changing human moods.

No masks are worn in the Balinese wayang wong plays. Their subjects are drawn from the *Ramayana*; those based on the *Mahabharata* and the *Bharatayuddha* (a Javanese epic poem based on the *Mahabharata*) are called *wayang parwa*.

The gamelan accompanies all these performances. Just as in Java there are several gamelan systems, depending on the occasion. However, there are important differences between Javanese and Balinese gamelan, both in the individual instruments and in the composition of the orchestra. Balinese music is much livelier than the Javanese; the gamelan is fuller and more melodious. As many as ten different types of gender may be used, producing a full sonorous tone.

Javanese dancing is of great antiquity, and once had a sacred meaning. It reached its zenith in the ceremonial Court dances at the Muslim kratons of Central Java. The influence of Islam is discernible in that these dances are performed during Muslim sacrificial festivals. The accompaniment is provided by the gamelan. A dalang speaks the introduction; and then male and female choruses sing. The dances are group performances, in which girls of noble birth, but not the daughters of the prince himself, took part. The dances are of two types: *bedaya*, performed by nine girls at a time, representing the nymphs of the goddess of the South Sea (i.e. the Java sea); and the *serimpi*, performed by a group of four girls, representing the heroines of a romance. The dances are highly stylized; every movement has its own meaning. They exhibit to perfection the qualities of Courtly dignity, complete self-control, and devotion to detail.

Balinese dances, though similar to the Javanese, are also more lively; as is the gamelan music itself. There are four main types: the *legong*, the *djanger*, the *sanghyan*, and the *ketjak*.

The legong is danced by two or three girls, whilst a dalang comments on each phase of the dance, and speaks the relevant parts. This dance requires several years of training. In the djanger two rows of men sit opposite one another, with the girl dancers forming the two other sides of a square. The actual dance itself takes place within the square, led by a man who is known as *dag*. In the sanghyans the girls dance in a state of ecstasy; it is believed that supernatural powers manifest themselves in the dancers. In the ketjak many male dancers take part; the dance portrays episodes which are taken from the *Ramayana*.

To turn to the present day, modern Indonesian drama lacks well-trained artists and experience in stage techniques. One type, known as the *komedi stambul*, introduced by a Eurasian at the end of the nineteenth century, has remained at the level of lower-class urban entertainment. A new development of this form, known as *sandiwara*, was sponsored by the Japanese cultural office during the occupation. Though it retains a certain popularity, it is far outclassed by the universal entertainment, the cinema.

The Indonesian film industry began about 1927 with very primitive productions, the early pictures being poor imitations of Dracula or Tarzan-type adventures and cheap love-stories. After the war, however, some Indonesian films were acclaimed internationally. One obstacle in the way of improvement is the fact that the upper-class audience in the towns measure Indonesian films against the best foreign productions. However, in late years the President has exerted himself to improve the situation by granting recognition to Indonesian film actors and actresses.

Plastic and Graphic Art

In sculpture there are, again, both traditional and Western forms. Most ethnic groups have had a traditional type of sculpture going back to prehistory. The later Hindu-Indonesian monuments show a highly developed sculpture. At the present day the art is best practised in Bali. There, sculpture in stone remains flourishing, with much carving being restored and new works being constantly produced. This is a result of the moral obligation on Balinese to maintain their temples in a proper state. Scenes both from mythology and from nature are depicted.

Akin to stone sculpture is wood-carving. This is to be found in Balinese homes; on the wooden supports of rice barns; and on gamelan instruments and their stands. Sculpture in wood has also flourished, the themes being taken from Hindu symbolism and the Hindu pantheon. These figures show very little feeling for space; usually they are frontal in style and as symmetrical as possible. They are ornamented in many colours, and to this owe their peculiar charm. In addition to the traditional sculptures, which restrict themselves to Hindu religious ideas, some profane figures are also found.

Bali's vigorous tradition was intimately linked with the religious life of the people, and it reacted strongly to modern developments. Largely as a result of the influence of the Mexican ethnologist and caricaturist Miguel Covarrubias, the sculptors turned to produce wood sculptures of very slender figures with elongated arms and without ornamentation, quite different from their traditional style. After this innovation, other forms and styles were developed which all strike a distinctly Balinese note.

Prehistoric cave-paintings are found in Indonesia. Since Islamic religious law prohibits representational art, the graphic arts (like the plastic) did not flourish in the Muslim period; no representative art survived, though puppets for the wayang continued to be made.

Traditional painting and drawing are found only in Java and Bali, in the flat leather wayang puppets. In addition, however, the Balinese decorate their walls with paintings on cloth, which represent scenes from mythology. In Bali, painting has remained a living art, unlike Java, where it was neglected after Islam achieved dominance. Balinese painting portrayed episodes from literary works, especially those inspired by Hinduism (the *Ramayana* and the *Bharatayuddha*).

Beginning in the mid nineteenth century, Indonesians began to paint in a European style. Balinese painting evolved along completely individual lines. Painters turned from the world of gods and demons to that of men. In form, paintings moved from the two- to the three-dimensional, though they remained prone to ornamentation, especially in the shape of trees and flowers. In Java, however, until the nineteen-twenties modern painters had little impact on Indonesian society, as they were quite divorced from traditional art. Thereafter, the European-style artists tried to increase their acceptance by training others to paint in their fashion. This school of artists was Javanese-centred, and accordingly held that the new culture should be a development of the past. Their work, however, was only brought to the attention of the people by the Japanese authorities during the occupation. With the outbreak of revolt against the Dutch and the subsequent achievement of independence, further support was given to the modern style. Especially important has been that from the President, who maintains in his palace in Djakarta a collection of the best of the paintings produced in recent years. It is well to note that Indonesian painting has grown to its present stature in the brief space of a few decades in a country which had known no individual art.

Ornamentation

Decorative art leans strongly towards traditional motifs; it has its roots in antiquity. The most highly developed decorations are those applied to textiles, and the best known of these are *ikat* and *batik*.

Ikat is a method of dyeing thread before weaving, which was brought to Indonesia by migrants from the Asian mainland in prehistoric times. Fibres are wound round small groups of threads at various places, so that the tightly bound parts do not take up the colour when the fabric is dipped into the dye-bath. Unfortunately, this art is rapidly dying, if not indeed dead, in face of the onslaught of manufactured textiles.

Batik is also a method of producing coloured designs on cloth, practised almost exclusively in Java and Madura. The parts of the cloth that are not to be dyed are covered with wax, applied with a funnel-shaped crucible. After the uncovered parts have been dyed, the wax is melted off in hot water, and the process continues until the design is complete.

The earliest batik fabrics had only a colourless drawing on a dark blue background. The dye used was indigo, for which Java was once famous. Later it became possible to use more than one colour.

In the principalities (Jogyakarta, Surakarta), the custodians of traditional culture, the preferred combination was indigo, soga brown (obtained from the bast of certain trees), and white. Outside the principalities yellow and red were also used. The art of dyeing red was introduced by Indian Muslims during the eighteenth century.

Batik is used to produce many articles of Javanese clothing. It is principally famous for the kain, or wrap-around cloth used to form a skirt, from waist to ankle, worn by all Javanese women and many Javanese men. But also the headkerchief or *ikat kepala* or *blangkon*, is batik, as is the shawl in which articles are carried, the *slendang*, and the breast covering used by women, the *kemben*.

When, in the nineteenth century, batik was faced with competition from the much cheaper imported textiles, a new method was created which took advantage of the repetitive character of batik designs. It consists of applying the pattern on to the fabric by means of copper stamps which have previously been impressed on a wax pad. Thus the 'repeats' in the pattern can be applied in wax by a single action. The Chinese set up a large number of workshops which produced this type of cloth, later to become known as *tjap* from the copper stamp used. It must be said that in beauty of appearance there is very little to distinguish tjap from batik; however, the fact that each batik is an individual production, which shows minor errors where the hand has slipped, and takes very much longer to make than tjap, gives it a scarcity and therefore commercial value perhaps out of proportion to its intrinsic artistic merits.

The interest of this development lies in the fact that it shows the vitality achieved in at least one form of cultural expression. By adapting the process of its production to the changed economic situation, batik manufacturers have ensured its propagation to more people than would ever have been possible had the craft remained entirely manual. The originators of the new method were Chinese-Indonesians; an indication that an indigenous artistic tradition may be saved from extinction by the enterprise of foreigners. We can only hope that, in one way or another, Indonesia's other cultural accomplishments will be able to survive the social and economic changes which lie ahead.

12   From Freedom to Xenophobia

The Factions

AS WE HAVE SEEN in preceding chapters, history has treated the
Javanese differently from the other ethnic groups. The former,
occupying Central and East Java, were the most Indianized, and
are among the least Muslim, of the peoples in the archipelago. Unlike
the Javanese, the other peoples have never developed a centralized,
authoritarian social system. Madjapahit had been the great Javanese
Empire; that of the peoples of South Sumatra had been Shrivijaya,
no despotic realm, but simply a great trading emporium – and a
constant rival of the Javanese states.

The Javanese also became the most closely governed by the Dutch,
who kept the other peoples on a much looser rein. In any case, the
latter (with the exception, of course, of the Moluccas) had had a
briefer experience of colonialism. To take an extreme contrast, the
Atjehnese of North Sumatra knew Dutch control for barely four
decades; some Javanese knew it for three centuries.

Given their history and social systems, the non-Javanese naturally
prefer social arrangements which permit them the maximum of
freedom. Their belief in the virtues of private trade is much greater
than that of the Javanese, for whom the ideal is service to the state.
The ideological framework of a non-Javanese is provided by an
outward-looking system of Islamic thought, not by the introverted
memories of the Javanese empire of centuries ago. He might not even
think of the Dutch (and therefore the West) as oppressors, but rather
as pacifiers of his predatory neighbours.

These differences in historical experience and outlook are bedevilled by economic disparities. It is here that the division between

180

the Javanese and the other peoples of Indonesia appears at its sharpest. For Java is the only island not producing more than it consumes; in fact, it absorbs the surplus of the other islands. Even Java's western third is more productive than Central and East Java, the homelands of the Javanese. Sumatra accounts for over two-thirds of Indonesia's exports by value; Java, with about two-thirds of the population, contributes only 15 per cent of the value of export earnings. In brief the other Indonesian peoples would undoubtedly be better off without the Javanese; the latter would be even poorer without them. It is the Javanese, therefore, who exert themselves most to retain the unity of Indonesia, and to deny the ethnic divisions. The other peoples, however, often distrust one another, especially if they are neighbours, as much as they do the Javanese. So that though the Javanese divide their support among three parties, these all see eye to eye, whilst the one party (the Masjumi) which claimed most of the political allegiances of the other-Indonesians was largely ineffective. Their ethnic and cultural differences prevented any joint action in defence of their economic interests.

Even in the pre-war nationalist movement the differences between Javanese and other-Indonesians had shown themselves. The parties favoured by Javanese tended to be made up of an *élite* leadership and a mass following, rather like Javanese society itself. Of this type had been the Sarekat Islam and the Communist Party, and the various non-co-operative parties in which Sukarno had been involved. Quite distinct were the parties led by Hatta and Sjahrir, both men Menang-kabau (Central Sumatra). These were based rather on the principle of informed participation by all members. Numbers were the strength of the Javanese parties; but when they lost their leaders, they collapsed. Hatta and Sjahrir's parties were small in number, but able continuously to produce new leadership.

With the disappearance of colonial pressure, Indonesian politics became a struggle between the parties backed mainly by the Javanese, whom we may call the Javanese faction, and those supported by the other-Indonesians. Not all those in the Javanese faction were Javanese; some were from other Indonesian peoples; just as there were some Javanese, in the revolts of 1958, who threw in their lot with the non-Javanese. It still remains true that most of those in the Javanese faction were Javanese; and the bulk of the non-Javanese factions were from other Indonesian ethnic groups. Given Indonesia's newness as a state, it would be strange if matters were otherwise.

The difficulty of keeping Indonesia together lies in the fact that its peoples are principally united by 'ties of common colonial experience', as President Sukarno put it.[13] This is a thread of diminishing strength to withstand the powerful pull of economic interest. More important have been the Javanese political strengths. Having been favoured by the Dutch with more modern education than any other of the Indonesian peoples, they have largely staffed the administration. Furthermore, since they were able to retain their organization intact against Dutch attack, they emerged from the struggle with their own armed forces. This was to prove decisive.

It must not be thought that Indonesians support policies which have as their sole aim and justification the retention of power by their own particular ethnic group. All motives are always mixed; policies which may be genuinely held to be in the best interests of the country may well require the holding of power by oneself, one's kin, and one's ethnic group. Even in advanced countries it is not unknown for associates of prime ministers or presidents to be related to them. In Indonesia the support of one's kin and ethnic group are likely to be important political motives for some time to come.

The consequence of the above is that when assessing, for example, 'democratic' arguments, one has to remember both that they may be genuine, and that they would not be held if those who supported them were differently situated. It would also be unwise to think that those who advance arguments for authoritarian government do so from sheer wrong-headedness; their position, economic and social, may make authoritarianism the preferred form of political organization.

Cold War

Once a unitary state was in being, the battle for control began. The first cabinet was composed mainly of the Masjumi, with one of its leaders, Mohammed Natsir, as Prime Minister. The Masjumi then, as well as being the most important party outside Java, also enjoyed undoubtedly the most widespread and largest support in the country. At the time it included the Nahdatul Ulama (Muslim Scholars) Party, an orthodox group which received nearly all its support from the homelands of the Javanese, and particularly East Java. However, it was opposed by the PNI (Nationalist Party) which was backed by the Javanese bureaucracy (and those they were able to control) and, most of all, by the President. He had a strong personal following among Javanese, and was then still held in high regard by the other peoples. In combination, they caused the fall of the cabinet in April 1951, after only eight months in office.

The next Prime Minister was a Dr Sukiman, a long-time nationalist. Though also a leader of the Masjumi, he was in addition a close associate of Sukarno, and a Javanese. He was able to create a cabinet based upon both the PNI and the Masjumi. However, its Foreign Minister signed an agreement with the USA which the cabinet's opponents portrayed as implying the abandonment of an independent foreign policy; it fell in April 1952.

The succeeding government was headed by Wilopo of the PNI, who collected round him a group of bright young men from both the PNI and the Masjumi. Unfortunately, they were somewhat inexperienced in politics. They attempted to reduce the Army to a less cumbrous and more efficient force, and so threatened to dismiss many of the Javanese guerrillas, who were the military support of the Javanese faction. These naturally opposed the proposed reorganization in Parliament; a demonstration followed, and was in turn succeeded by intrigues in the Army. The cabinet's fate was thus sealed, and it resigned on 1 August 1953.

The Javanese faction's political arms had been predominantly the PNI and the President, Sukarno. However, the PNI was mainly backed by the Javanese bureaucracy; it had little support at village level. The NU's ethnic basis and conservative religious beliefs combined to urge it to leave the modernist Masjumi; it did so in mid 1952. Then, the communists were given a free hand; in return they changed their policy from revolution to support of Sukarno's nationalism. Thus the bureaucracy was able to acquire village-level support in East Java through the NU, and a peasant and urban-worker base generally in Java through the PKI (Communist Party).

So the battle-lines were drawn. On one side were the parties of the Javanese faction: the PNI, the NU, the PKI, and President Sukarno. On the other were elements of the other-Indonesian factions: the Masjumi; the small but able PSI (Socialist Party) led by *Sutan* Sjahrir; and Vice-President Hatta, whose political weight, however, was and is much inferior to the President's, for both personal and official reasons. There was now no party which had strong support among both Javanese and other-Indonesians, though the Masjumi was better supported across the country than any other.

The next cabinet included only the Javanese faction. Its main component was the PNI, one of whose leaders, Ali Sastroamidjojo, was Prime Minister. The NU was included in the cabinet; the Masjumi and the Socialists were in opposition. The cabinet in-augurated the rule of inefficiency and corruption which has continued to gain strength ever since. However, enjoying the support of both President and communists, it remained in power longer than any previous cabinet, from August 1953 to August 1955. Needless to say, the trend of events was not lost on the other-Indonesians, as the actions of the dissident movements soon showed.

The Atjehnese of the northern tip of Sumatra, as we have seen, had a long and fierce history of opposition to foreign rule. When Japanese control ended, the Islamic teachers seized power and Atjeh became a province under their control. However, in 1950 it lost its provincial status. This was bad enough, but in addition the Ali cabinet, immediately after taking office, ruled that Atjeh was no longer to trade direct with Singapore. This of course really meant that the Atjehnese were now to work for the Javanese. The whole of the territory rose in revolt, and its leader (and Governor when it had been a province) Daud Beureuh, declared that Atjeh was hence-forth part of the Islamic State of Indonesia. The rebellion subsided only when, over the years, Atjeh was given virtual autonomy in finance. The core of the Islamic state was the Darul Islam. This was a movement formed of those who had been the military wing of the

Masjumi in West Java. In March 1948, when it was not clear that the Republic of Indonesia would survive the imminent Dutch attack, they had declared their own state in West Java. They appear to have been, and to have been supported by, Sundanese people of West Java. They maintained their armed opposition until 1962.

In South Celebes, one of the fighters against Dutch colonialism, Kahar Muzakkar, had later helped in the imposition of unitary rule. He had then found it insufficiently Islamic for his tastes, and had decamped with his followers to the hills. They had acquired control over most of the countryside outside Makassar itself. He did not wait as long as the Atjehnese; shortly after the Ali cabinet took office, on 7 August 1953, he declared his territory officially part of the Islamic state of Indonesia. (Early in 1965 he was reported killed.)

What Islam has meant to its followers has depended on time, place, and circumstance. In the Netherlands Indies it has been used both by the Atjehnese and by the Javanese Prince Diponegoro as a rallying-cry against the Dutch. In present-day Indonesia it similarly serves as a banner of opposition to rule by the Javanese faction. The modernist Masjumi as well as the orthodox Darul Islam and its allies, strongly supported by non-Javanese, oppose the Javanese faction. Of course, just as many Muslim divines had been quite satisfied with colonial rule, so also the orthodox Nahdatul Ulama, forming part of the Javanese faction, has found little fault with the dispensation of power and privilege in Indonesia.

In an attempt by the Javanese faction to suggest that all these dissident movements were Dutch (and therefore 'colonialist') in inspiration, a number of Dutchmen were arrested in December 1953 and January 1954, and detained for considerable periods. No evidence was ever produced in support of the government allegations, and the main result of this exercise was further to embitter relations with the Netherlands.

In the Ali cabinet the pattern of rule of the Javanese faction became apparent. An external enemy was to be found against whom animosity was to be aroused, whilst the faction built up its power at home. In August 1954 the government asked that the question of Western New Guinea be placed on the agenda for the next General

Assembly of the United Nations. It sought to obtain that body's support for a demand that the Dutch negotiate, with the prerequisite that they be willing to surrender sovereignty. In this the government failed, and it then turned to organize xenophobia at home. In April of 1955 it acted as host to the Bandung Conference. The main themes at this Conference were anti-West and anti-White; it supported the claim to Western New Guinea.

Inefficient and corrupt though the cabinet may have been, it still accomplished its main purpose: to cripple the chances of the Masjumi in the long-delayed elections. It appointed its loyal supporters to strategic posts in the internal administration. The President in turn compelled the PNI and therefore the government, somewhat against their will, to grant facilities to the communists and to turn a blind eye to their methods. However, when Sukarno failed to install his own man as Chief of Staff of the Army, the cabinet fell, and the President went on pilgrimage to Mecca.

The next cabinet took office in August 1955, during Sukarno's absence, and included the Masjumi and the NU, as well as the socialists and others. Its achievement was to show that not even a common religion was enough to bridge the gap between Javanese and others. For the NU would not co-operate with its co-religionists of the non-Javanese faction, while the remainder of the Javanese faction (President, PNI, and the communists) were naturally hostile. The cabinet acquired popularity by hounding corruption, but was in office too briefly before the elections of September 1955 (the only ones ever to have taken place) to undo the harm done by the previous cabinet. The results revealed that the Masjumi had received somewhat less votes than the PNI. The cabinet turned into a caretaker, and resigned in March 1956.

The communists had obtained an unexpectedly large vote in the elections. This impelled the PNI to co-operate sufficiently with the Masjumi to form a government, which included the NU but not the communists. The Prime Minister was again Ali Sastroamidjojo. However, as a result of the system of proportional representation used for the elections, the Javanese faction, which previously had been in the minority, now had an absolute majority in Parliament.

In consequence, not even fear of the communists ensured co-operation with the non-Javanese faction. Matters took their course: inefficiency and corruption at home; animosity to the foreigner abroad. The only ones to benefit were the communists, who waxed in strength while criticizing the cabinet, especially, of course, the Masjumi.

In April 1956 the government abrogated the still-born Netherlands-Indonesian Union set up by The Hague Agreement; in August the debts assumed under that treaty were repudiated. In the same month an All-Indonesia People's Congress was held to arouse popular support favouring the demand for Western New Guinea. Two months later that issue was again placed on the agenda of the United Nations General Assembly.

All this contrived xenophobia failed to silence the other-Indonesians. In November a former Chief of Staff, Colonel Zulkifli Lubis, launched an abortive *coup* against the government. Most, if not all, of those involved were not Javanese. More serious expressions of discontent were in the making. The regions outside Java were becoming rather tired of seeing their railways become unusable and their roads become potholes, so that cash crops could be transported only on a man's back, while the railways and roads of unproductive Java were kept in good repair. Despite the fact that they earned most of Indonesia's foreign exchange, the Central government neither maintained their facilities nor permitted them to do so themselves. In addition, they resented the fact that the Javanese bureaucracy was expanding into their territories, denying their own young men opportunities of entering government service. They saw no reason why the Javanese should relieve their own problem of educated unemployment at the expense of the other peoples. The subordinate position of the Masjumi, the party they supported in the cabinet, prevented it from doing anything to alleviate their distress.

Though the civilians were powerless, the military were not. The army commanders outside Java were not being provided with enough money to pay their men nor sufficient rice to feed them. Those in Celebes and North Sumatra accordingly began to barter copra and rubber in Singapore for what they needed; which of course deprived the Javanese faction of foreign exchange.

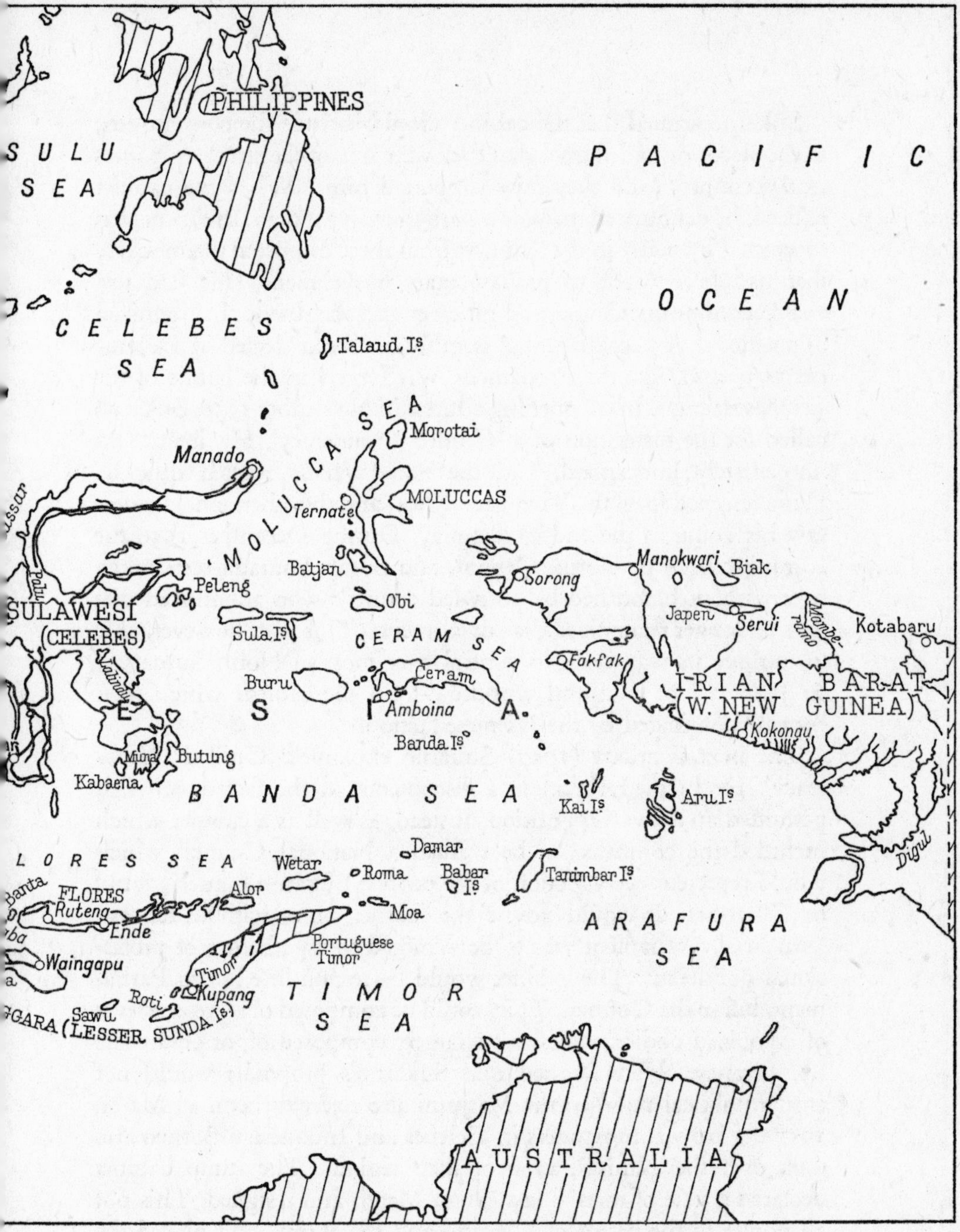

Political map of Indonesia

Sukarno argued that the cabinet should include the communists, as the elections had shown that they were one of the strongest parties in the country (and they now supported him). When the cabinet refused, he denounced the whole parliamentary system. In this he was supported by many in the country, from sheer disgust at the mockery that had been made of parliamentary government. (He had just visited communist China, and much envied the absence of organized opposition.) A Constituent Assembly had been elected in December 1955 and, like the Parliament, was largely in the hands of the Javanese faction. In his opening address in November 1956, Sukarno called for the institution of a 'Guided Democracy'. His intent was immediately understood, and the non-Javanese reacted quickly. Hatta resigned from the Vice-Presidency, and the other non-Javanese saw his going as the end of fair play. During December 1956 the administrations of North, Central, and South Sumatra were taken over without bloodshed by army-led councils who announced that they no longer recognized the government. (This was, however, able to intrigue its way back to control over most of North Sumatra.) In January, the Masjumi withdrew from the cabinet which then became dominated by the Javanese faction.

The next February (1957) Sukarno explained 'Guided Democracy'. He blamed Indonesia's discontents on the fact that it had permitted an active Opposition. Instead, as well as a cabinet which included the communists, he wanted a National Council which would represent every section of the people; Sukarno himself would be Chairman. It would 'advise' the cabinet, on or without request.

In brief, Parliament was to be demoted to a gathering of professional politicians. The cabinet would be responsible not to Parliament, but to the Council. This would be composed of representatives of organized bodies, which were largely composed of, or controlled by, Javanese. Hatta argued that Sukarno's proposals would not ensure political stability; the Masjumi also rejected them. In March 1957 the army commanders in Celebes and Indonesian Borneo also took over the administration of their regions. The rump cabinet declared a state of martial law on 14 March and resigned. This put all power in the hands of Sukarno and the Army, and placed the commanders of the Javanese units on a par with those of non-Javanese formations.

The non-Javanese now demanded that Hatta be appointed to form a new cabinet; but Sukarno was not interested in government by consent. After one of his nominees from the PNI had failed to form a cabinet, he undertook the task himself, and assembled a group of twenty-three oddly assorted people, with Djuanda Karta-widjaja, a non-party man, as Prime Minister. The cabinet was of course based on the non-communist parties of the Javanese faction, and supported by the communists in Parliament. The Masjumi refused to take part. The cabinet's inauguration in April 1957 signalled the beginning of the end of parliamentary government (it was never democracy) in Indonesia. The next month Sukarno set up his National Council. It included several important groups, which were described as 'regional and functional'; the latter term included the armed forces, farmers, labour, religious groups, and co-operatives. These were predominantly Javanese; there was no formal Opposition. All members were directly or indirectly selected by the President: the Council was responsible only to him, and he, as ever, to nobody.

Civil Strife

A new, and sinister, note now began to be struck. The various political parties, youth groups, ex-servicemen's associations, trade unions, etc., through which the Javanese faction emits its trial balloons began to demand drastic action if the United Nations did not back the Indonesian demand. In September 1957 the Prime Minister attempted to stop the rot by calling a national conference to which he invited prominent regional military and civilian leaders, including Hatta as well as of course Sukarno. It came to nothing, as Sukarno was unwilling to give Hatta any considerable role in government.

Events began to move towards a climax. In October Sukarno demanded drastic measures against Dutch nationals and property; the next month a mass rally was organized in Djakarta urging the same proposals.

These political antics cut very little ice with the autonomous regions outside Java. They continued to appropriate foreign exchange, demanded that Sukarno reconcile himself to Hatta, and that the latter be installed in a leading position in government. The rift between Sukarno and the Masjumi widened. The Javanese faction attempted to pacify the other islanders by giving them very large subsidies, by conceding the years-old demand for more decentralization, and by intrigue; it achieved little success.

On 29 November 1957 the United Nations rejected the Indonesian demand; on the 30th an attempt was made on Sukarno's life, and on the next day the government authorized the seizure of Dutch business firms by gangs of young men, often communist-led, and Dutch people were denied services or food of any kind. It also ordered the expulsion of the majority of Netherlands nationals in the country, who were mostly Eurasians who had known no home but Indonesia. The 500 Dutch-owned estates and plantations were placed under government, that is to say military control; all seized properties were formally nationalized about a year later.

Among the Dutch properties taken was the inter-island shipping company, the KPM. Traffic between the islands in consequence virtually came to a standstill, and famine conditions prevailed in several parts of Java and East Indonesia. (The government was eventually compelled to return the ships to their owners.)

The Javanese faction had in this way successfully applied the techniques taught them by the Japanese several years earlier. Many of the young men produced by the rapidly expanding educational system had been found jobs, and no matter where their origins, their support for the Javanese faction was assured. With the former Dutch plantations under its control, the Army had its long-wanted assurance of supplies. Thus, in a very material sense, sanctions against the foreigner were used to build up support at home. The instigator of these actions had been President Sukarno. With their successful completion, he left on a foreign tour.

A number of democratic Indonesian leaders, after being threatened by the youth organizations of the Javanese faction, had taken refuge in Central Sumatra. Among them were Mohammed Natsir, the former Prime Minister and Chairman of the Masjumi, Sumitro Djojohadikusumo, a Socialist leader, and Shaffruddin Prawirane gara, Governor of the country's central bank and also a leader of the Masjumi. Together with the leaders of the autonomous province, they formed a Revolutionary Council.

In January 1958 the government ordered the Navy to ensure that the autonomous regions stopped barter trade with Singapore and the Philippines, despite the fact that the dislocation of the transport system had cut them off from Java. The next month the Council gave Sukarno an ultimatum, demanding that he dismiss the cabinet within five days, abandon 'Guided Democracy', and appoint a new government headed by Hatta and the Sultan of Jogyakarta.

The Council had hoped that it would receive help from the other non-Javanese territories. But here the divisions between the other Indonesians showed themselves; only North Celebes rallied to the Council's support. Sukarno returned in mid February, and a week later ordered the Army to suppress the revolt. Javanese numbers and unity carried the day. Paradoxically, there was very little resistance to overcome in Central Sumatra, the centre of the revolt, where the last rebel stronghold was taken on 22 May 1958, and only in North Celebes was there fierce fighting. Even there it ended in September of the same year.

The consequences of the rebellion for the Indonesian state were more important than the revolt itself. The rebels had asserted that they had no intention of destroying the unity of the country; they were fighting for democracy and against communism. Since this agreed with their interests, there is no reason to disbelieve them. The United States government accordingly lent them a certain degree of support, rapidly withdrawn when they began to lose. The assistance given was not, of course, sufficient to ensure victory (given the discrepancy in numbers between the two sides this was in any case unlikely), but it was quite enough to help the Javanese faction in their arms hunting expeditions. To the communist block it appeared that the rebels were the tools of American imperialism; to the 'non-aligned' that arms were necessary to maintain Indonesia's independence from the power groupings. In consequence, arms came from Yugoslavia,

Czechoslovakia, and the Soviet Union, from India and Egypt, and on a commercial basis from Western Germany. Success forgives all, and when the Javanese faction were clearly winning, the United States agreed to supply light military equipment.

In the Javanese mind the West's attitude confirmed the impression that no good could come from it. In consequence, that faction was only too glad to intensify its courtship of the Soviet Union. The revolt marked the beginning of the process whereby that country has become, in fact if not in form, the patron of Indonesia. It need not be supposed to favour the Javanese faction; it merely wishes to reduce Western influence. Since, however, it is the Javanese who are similarly inclined, the Soviet Union supports them.

In its turn the Javanese faction has used the fact of Soviet support to maximum advantage in its dealings with the West. Having courted the Soviet Union abroad and built up the Communist Party at home, the faction presents both as threats to compel the West to placate Indonesian demands. To accept this argument is to ignore the internal compulsions which would in any case make the Javanese faction hew to the totalitarian line.

Despotism

With military superiority assured, there was no reason for the Javanese faction to tolerate any genuine representation of the other Indonesian peoples, and in July 1959 President Sukarno dissolved the Constituent Assembly. It had been on the point of reaching a decision in favour of a bicameral constitution, with the Upper House to ensure regional representation. This did not please Sukarno. He intervened and asked the Assembly to accept the still-born Constitution of 1945, which had prescribed a strong Presidential cabinet. The Constituent Assembly refused; he sent it home, and decreed the Constitution, which gave him, and not an elected cabinet, supreme powers. He then renamed the National Council as the Supreme Advisory Council provided for in that Constitution. Decentralization was abruptly cancelled, government became more centralized than ever before; and the Javanese bureaucracy flowed into the other islands in increasing numbers.

Sukarno's idea of 'Guided Democracy' involved creating debating chambers modelled on the National Council he had created in May 1957, with all members directly or indirectly selected by the government, i.e. the President. In March 1960 the elected Parliament was replaced by a 'Mutual Help' Parliament. The Masjumi and the PSI were excluded, the other political parties were treated as if they were a professional group, rather than representatives of the people, and were given half the seats. A year later Sukarno ordained that only eight political parties were to exist; the Masjumi and the PSI were not among them. No votes were to be taken in the Mutual Help Parliament; in case of disagreement Sukarno would decide. In 1961 regional assemblies were established on the same formula. 'Guided Democracy' had come into being.

Having taken over the property and jobs of the Dutch, the Javanese faction now cast covetous eyes on the Chinese. Of these, the most vulnerable were those who followed the Kuo Min Tang refugee government in Taiwan; they came on to the anvil first. On the assertion that Nationalist China had helped the rebels in Sumatra, many Chinese in Djakarta were arrested, all KMT organizations were banned, and all their schools and business firms were placed under government control. (Although an American soldier of fortune had been captured flying for the rebels, needless to say no measures were taken against Americans!)

Less than a year later, in September 1959, it was the turn of the communist Chinese. The People's Republic of China had been more than willing to settle the matter of the nationality of Chinese in Indonesia. However, the Indonesian government, in the hands of the Javanese faction, dragged its feet and did not ratify a treaty signed in April 1955, for what reasons one can only guess. In September 1959 the government decreed that all foreign traders were to move out of rural areas, and ordered them to sell their business to Indonesian citizens or co-operatives. (Due to the slowness of ratification of the treaty, few Chinese had been able to become Indonesian citizens.) A number of incidents occurred in which the Chinese Embassy was involved. Tension arose between the People's Republic of China and Indonesia, which was resolved only by the former's acceptance of the decree. The treaty was ratified the following year.

As was admitted at the time, the policy followed towards the Chinese was similar to that against the Dutch; the motive forces arose from Indonesian circumstances. The Javanese faction, faced with the need to provide loaves and fishes for its followers, unable to increase the productivity of the economy, resorted to a transfer of wealth from the more productive to the less. It thereby gained politi/ cal support, even from among the non-Javanese; unfortunately its actions only made the economic situation worse, and created a new need to satisfy the government's supporters. It was duly met. After the Dutch and the Chinese, the next to be 'socialized' were true/ blooded Indonesians. The government took over all import and exports, and put them in the hands of state corporations staffed with their Javanese supporters, so forcing out of business some 3,400 out of the 4,000 Indonesian importers.

As supreme body a People's Consultative Assembly was created. Parliament was included as a 'functional group'. The Assembly met for the first time in November and December 1960, and took two decisions. The first was to confer the title of 'Great Leader of the Revolution' on Sukarno; the second was to form a National Front to stir up the populace about Western New Guinea.

To guide the people, Sukarno also introduced a number of slogans, including USDEK, MANIPOL, and NEKAD, and took measures to ensure that all Indonesians absorbed them. MANIPOL stands for the Political Manifesto in which Sukarno explains his ideas on 'Guided Democracy'. USDEK is made up of the initial letters of five statements of principle in the manifesto, namely: return to the 1945 Constitution, Indonesian socialism, guided democracy, guided economy, Indonesian identity. Similarly, NEKAD stands for the goals of maintaining the unitary form of the republic, socialist republic, restoration of security, supporting religious faith, and loyalty to democratic principles. This signalled the beginning of an increasingly oppressive form of thought control, which has made tame parrots of the newspapers, eliminated all serious intellectual discussion in the country, and ruined the civil service. Only inefficiency has limited the extent of Indonesia's totalitarianism. Emphasis on ideology has helped incompetent demagogues to unseat the efficient in all fields: academic, administrative, and military. This has helped much in the decline of Indonesia's economy, as recorded in an earlier chapter.

The formal changes simply provided a cover for the fact that the Javanese faction, headed by Sukarno, was now firmly in control. Its main components are the bureaucracy, which is interwoven with the Nationalist Party and, in the Ministry for Religious Affairs, with the Nahdatul Ulama; the P K I; and the Army. All these bodies do not see eye to eye on everything, of course, but they are agreed on the need to keep down the other Indonesians. The bureaucracy is far from being a united body; rather it consists of a number of private empires, much as did its German Nazi counterpart. The Javanese faction, however, is also inefficient, nepotistic, and corrupt. Nevertheless, command over it is essential for control of the country, especially since victory over the rebels meant that there was now no obstacle to the bureaucracy's further spread into the other islands. To remain in charge, Sukarno has been playing off the P K I against the Army. For this reason, and also because, though no communist, he subscribes to many communist beliefs, practices, and goals, Sukarno has been concerned to maintain the strength of the P K I. The Army, though not averse to authoritarianism, does not intend to be dominated by the communists. It has occasionally snapped at them, but has been quickly brought to heel by Sukarno, unless of course the communists happened to be criticizing him; this was rare. As a consequence of the rebellion's failure, the influence of the militantly non-Javanese components of the Army has been quite eliminated; it therefore no longer shows any ability to stand up to the President. To shield themselves against the Army, the communists have been using Sukarno's need of them whilst steadily infiltrating into the society at large and into the Army itself. How long this triumvirate will remain so balanced is an open question. The Nahdatul Ulama's function is purely symbolic: mainly to permit Sukarno to say that religion was represented in the faction. This party is, so to speak, Islam domesticated for Javanese purposes.

Expansion

The new régime set itself three goals: pacification of the country; incorporation of Western New Guinea; and provision of enough food and clothing. By a flexible policy of force and persuasion, the Army largely achieved the first task. By the end of 1961, most of the 1958 rebels had 'returned to the Republic', as the official phrase had it; in some places this meant they replaced government forces as the legitimate authority. In mid 1962 the Darul Islam rebels in West Java, active since 1949, surrendered.

In consequence, the Indonesian Army was increasingly able to concentrate its energies on the Western New Guinea campaign and, emboldened by the flood of Soviet arms coming into the country, the Javanese faction embarked on an aggressive policy. In April 1960 President Sukarno visited both the United States and the Soviet Union, but was not able to change American neutrality on the issue. In May an organized mob stormed the Netherlands Legation in Djakarta. A month later all Dutch shipping was banned from Indonesian waters. On 17 August Sukarno broke off diplomatic relations with the Netherlands. In December he ordered the country to mobilize in readiness for the liberation of the territory. Towards the end of the year submarines, cruisers, and other warships acquired from Yugoslavia and Poland arrived in Djakarta. In January 1961 an Indonesian delegation visited Moscow and signed an agreement for the purchase of more arms to the value of $400 million, and obtained Soviet support for its claim to Western New Guinea.

The Netherlands would agree to a transfer of Western New Guinea to Indonesia only if the inhabitants were given the chance of self-determination. Since most of the people there were in fact Stone Age tribesmen, there was little sincerity in this proviso, which, Indonesia in any case refused to accept. It knew very well that to permit free choice to one part of the ex-Dutch Indies would be an invitation for others to claim the same, a possibility the government could not afford to contemplate. Early in 1962 the Netherlands dropped its condition; Indonesia nevertheless still refused to parley unless its sovereignty over the territory was first recognized.

In the middle of January 1962 Indonesian torpedo-boats were fired upon as they tried to break into Western New Guinea territorial waters. In the ensuing air of crisis, several political leaders of the dissolved Masjumi and PSI were arrested. Hatta sent a strongly worded, but ineffective, letter of protest to Sukarno, who declared general mobilization in the following month.

The United States now intervened, and both the Netherlands and Indonesia agreed to hold preliminary talks with an American mediator. (In February and again in May 1962 Russia agreed to sell more weapons to Indonesia.) Finally, at the beginning of June, both sides agreed to negotiate on the basis of a plan drawn up by the go-between, Mr Ellsworth Bunker, which provided that adminis-trative authority in Western New Guinea would be transferred to the United Nations. The formal agreement was signed on 15 August after a few hundred Indonesian paratroops had been dropped into the jungles of the territory. A cease-fire was called immediately; the United Nations assumed control on 1 October, and Indonesia took over from the UN on 1 May 1963, despite attempts by President Sukarno to have the date advanced. Diplomatic relations were resumed with the Netherlands on the same day. Indonesia promised to hold a plebiscite before the end of 1969 to enable the Papuan inhabitants to decide the future status of Western New Guinea. In November, however, President Sukarno declared that he wished to dispense with the plebiscite. Shortly after assuming control Indonesia placed the territory in quarantine, nobody being allowed in or out without a special permit.

The belated acquisition of Western New Guinea did nothing to resolve Indonesia's conflicts or lack of productivity, and another enemy was found. Towards the end of 1962, shortly after the Netherlands relinquished control over Western New Guinea, President Sukarno broadcast a call for help to a revolt which had broken out in Brunei. This began his continuous opposition to the plan to form a Federation of Malaysia from Malaya, Singapore, and the British Borneo territories. After many acrimonious exchanges with the Malayan Prime Minister, Tunku Abdul Rahman, they met in Tokyo at the end of May 1963 and resolved to try to settle their differences in a spirit of goodwill. However, when the agree- ment creating Malaysia was signed in London on 8 July, Sukarno accused the Tunku of 'breaking his word'. This was denied by the Tunku, and indeed no agreement not to go ahead with Malaysia was ever made public by either party.

President Sukarno, nevertheless, met the Tunku and President Macapagal of the Philippines in Manila from 30 July to 5 August. They decided to ask for, and to accept, a United Nations verifi- cation of whether the people in British North Borneo and Sarawak wanted to join Malaysia, and resolved to establish a 'Maphilindo' confederation of their three states. Accordingly, the United Nations carried out a survey and announced on 14 September that most people in the two territories concerned did indeed want to form part of Malaysia. But Sukarno was not able to give up an external enemy so easily, and he refused to recognize the new state when it came into being two days later. Malaya, therefore, broke off diplomatic relations with Indonesia; Djakarta mobs stormed the Malayan and burnt the British Embassy, and destroyed British property; a crowd in Kuala Lumpur burnt part of the Indonesian Embassy. British subjects and other foreigners were evacuated from Indonesia. Following the Dutch precedent, labour unions seized four British firms, which were taken over by government 'supervisory commissions'.

All traffic to and from Malaysia was suspended, and on 10 October Indonesia declared that it would establish four free ports and three free-trade zones in order to harm Malaysia. At the same time, it reduced to eight the number of ports from which goods could be exported. Indonesian Borneo, which accounts for 14 per cent of Indonesian exports, was only permitted a temporary port. These measures were intended to arrest the widespread smuggling and so to ensure that the produce of the other islands passed only through government hands. Given the accelerating inflation, it is unlikely that they will be successful: to the extent that they are, they simply cut off Indonesia's nose to spite her face.

Two thousand men, or one-sixth of the troops situated in Indo- nesian Borneo, and two battalions from Sumatra, were moved to the border with Sarawak. Guerrilla activity was concentrated in the centre and west. Raids were made by ever larger groups, eventually amounting to between sixty and a hundred men at a time. They were composed of young Chinese from urban areas in Sarawak, trained by the Indonesian Army, with regular Indonesian NCOs in charge, and helped by small units of Indonesian paratroopers. One of their principal objects was to link up with communist Chinese around Sibu in Sarawak and set up a 'government'; in this they failed. In the north of the island, in Sabah, Indonesian agents tried with no great success to build up a fifth column among the 17,000 Indonesians employed, mostly non-Javanese. In November General Nasution, the armed forces Chief of Staff, declared that Indonesia had in principle accepted Malaysia as a *fait accompli*. Sukarno, however, continued to chant that Malaysia must be crushed. That same month Dr Djuanda, the Prime Minister, died. The President appointed himself also Prime Minister, and reshuffled his Ministers to downgrade Nasution and, with him, the armed forces.

In December 1963 the communist organ in Djakarta published what became the Javanese faction's strategy in its anti-Malaysia campaign. It was a discussion by the Secretary-General of the Party, D. N. Aidit, of three approaches to the Malaysia 'problem'. He rejected the reformist solution, which expected the British and Malaysians to settle peacefully. Equally unwelcome was the second, adventurist, approach (which by implication was the launching of a war); this would provoke British attack, create panic in Indonesia, and topple Sukarno. The only correct approach was the 'revolutionary' one, which required a long-drawn-out confrontation in all fields, appeals for sympathy to 'new emerging forces', recognition of the North Borneo rebel movement, and expropriation of British enterprises.[14] Eight months after this statement, in his 1964 Independence Day speech, Sukarno translated this view into his own language by declaring that the revolution went from confrontation to confrontation.

Late in January 1964 the United States Attorney-General, Robert Kennedy, attempted to achieve a settlement of the dispute in visits to Sukarno, Macapagal, and the Tunku. He managed to persuade

Sukarno to decree a cease-fire, but hardly had he left Djakarta than President Sukarno declared that his policy was still to crush Malaysia. The Foreign Ministers of the three States met in Bangkok in February, and agreed that Thailand would supervise the cease-fire. Less than four weeks later overt fighting began again.

In May, General Nasution announced that volunteers (some said 21 million of them) were being mobilized. Sukarno issued an 'Action Command', and it was announced that a 'brigade' of these volunteers would be accompanied to the Kalimantan border by regular troops, preparatory to entering Malaysian territory. Training centres were set up in various islands near Singapore. Indonesian-trained communist Chinese from Singapore and the Peninsula were sent back there for sabotage.

In the same month the Philippines entered upon an attempt to make peace between Indonesia and Malaysia. Having publicly announced that Malaysia would be 'totally crushed' by 1 January 1965, Sukarno then conceded in private discussion with a Philippines special envoy that he would be prepared to withdraw some of his forces from Malaysian Borneo prior to a meeting of the Heads of State of Indonesia, Malaysia, and the Philippines.

Malaysia demanded that this withdrawal be substantial, and that agreement be reached on eventual total withdrawal, irrespective of the outcome of the talks. Indonesia was only prepared to make a token withdrawal of her forces from Malaysian territory, with total evacuation dependent on the progress of the political discussions. A summit meeting was, nevertheless, held in Tokyo in June. Tunku Abdul Rahman demanded that all acts of hostility should cease; Sukarno refused, and the talks collapsed. That the Indonesians had no intention of reaching agreement was obvious from the fact that never in the weeks of preparation for the meeting was there any lessening of Indonesian activities in Malaysian Borneo.

In July 1964, Mr Anastas Mikoyan, then Soviet Deputy Prime Minister, visited Indonesia and reaffirmed Soviet support for Indonesian hostilities towards Malaysia. A series of landings began by sea and by air of Indonesian guerrillas on the Malayan Peninsula proper (which Indonesia had recognized as independent since 1957).

With the assistance of the local population, the invaders were quickly killed or captured. Malaysia finally complained of Indonesian aggression to the Security Council. In September, of the eleven members, nine (including the two Afro-Asians, Ivory Coast and Morocco) voted in favour of a Norwegian motion deploring the Indonesian action; the Soviet Union, however, exercised its veto.

Towards the end of August, Sukarno reshuffled his cabinet, for the first time appointing to it a communist, Nyoto, who was Deputy Chairman of his party. The President thus finally achieved his ambition of forming a NASAKOM cabinet, which incorporated what he considered the three main forces: Nationalism, Religion, and Communism. The Communist Party was by far the largest political party in Indonesia; at the end of June 1963 it claimed to have 3 million members, in addition to some 14 million belonging to various front organizations. Internationally the party was emphatically pro-Chinese. Not surprisingly, after Nyoto's appointment, Indonesian foreign policy shifted to the Chinese variant of the communist line. This was especially marked at the Cairo Non-Aligned Conference in October 1964, where Indonesia had the largest delegation, in an obvious attempt to repair the damage done to her reputation by the Security Council vote. Sukarno struck Chinese poses, calling for world-wide hostilities against 'neo-colonialism', but did not achieve much; the tone of the Conference was set by moderate opinion. He had been no more successful during a visit to Moscow on his way to Cairo, when he had asked for more arms. His hosts agreed to little other than a postponement of payment for those they had already supplied.

In the meantime the seizure of British firms continued and by April 1964 most of them were under either government or union control. In May, on a public suggestion from the Supreme Advisory Council, the government began to expropriate British firms; compensation was not mentioned.

British interests had thus been treated similarly to Dutch and Chinese in previous years. Simultaneously, however, the government had been exerting itself to improve its relations with the Netherlands. Diplomatic links were restored in March 1963, sea communications in June, in July commerce recommenced and a Dutch trade mission visited Indonesia. The first official commercial contract was signed in November between a Dutch firm and an Indonesian state electrical undertaking. In April 1964 a technical co-operation agreement was reached, covering the exchange of equipment, personnel, and technical and scientific knowledge. After a visit by the Dutch Foreign Minister, Dr Luns, to Djakarta in July, it was agreed that the Netherlands government would grant an export credit of $30 million for 1965, that the Netherlands claims for compensation were to be discussed by various commissions, and that commerce which had been diverted to Malaysia during the anti-Dutch campaign would revert to the Netherlands, as well as some of the trade in Indonesian tobacco and tea which had been channelled to West Germany and Belgium. Netherlands subjects were to be allowed to return to Indonesia under certain conditions.

Indonesia's bellicosity, however, alarmed those countries which for some time had been carrying on a one-sided courtship with her. Britain, Australia, and New Zealand now gave specific promises to defend Malaysia against aggression, and the first-named stopped its Colombo Plan aid to Indonesia. The United States suspended all aid, with the sole exception of surplus farm products. This called forth the comment 'To hell with all foreign aid that has strings attached to it . . .' from Sukarno. France announced early in 1964 that no more contracts for arms would be signed with Indonesia. In April of that year the Australian Defence Minister announced that military aid to Malaysia would be increased beyond the £3 million already promised, and that the first Australian troops would be sent to Borneo. British, Australian, and New Zealand troops assisted Malaysian forces in eliminating Indonesian troops who either infil-trated across the Malaysian border in Borneo or were landed in the Peninsula. Finally, in November 1964, Australia for the first time in her history adopted peace-time conscription to face up to the Indonesian threat.

It is time to review the record of the Javanese faction's rule. They had succeeded in incorporating Western New Guinea into the Republic, as they had promised. They had also largely pacified the country; though South Celebes continued to give trouble. But in their third aim, that of providing food and clothing to the people, they had failed disastrously. The cost of living had soared to ever new peaks: in the capital, Djakarta, the consumer index had risen twenty-one times between 1958 and April 1964:[15] thus measuring very accurately the erosion of living standards of the urban population since the advent of 'Guided Democracy'.

It used to be argued, both by Indonesian officials and others, that half the population was protected from monetary inflation by reason of the fact that it subsisted by barter. However, even this shield was pierced by the general incompetence of the régime. In February 1964 the Deputy-Governor of Central Java estimated that 1 million people were starving after the longest drought and worst rat plague in living memory.[16]

This failure in the agricultural field was a direct result of the inadequate investments made in it. For though, as recorded in a previous chapter, a large quantity of foreign aid has come to Indonesia, it has been used primarily to ensure support for the Javanese faction whilst reducing their dependence on the other Indonesians. Neither need nor efficiency have been as potent arguments for help as political importance. So the peasantry, who needed assistance most, got least, while the principal recipients were the armed forces, the bureaucracy, and other urban-dwellers. Among other privileges, they were able to buy rice at subsidized rates. With the famine conditions prevalent in many parts of Java in early 1964, however, the government was forced to follow Sukarno's retort to criticism, 'Let them eat maize', and diluted the rice ration accordingly. Even this proved impossible to maintain, and in September 1964 it was decided to give the privileged categories the monetary equivalent, at ruling prices, of the rice the government would otherwise have provided at subsidized rates. In brief, the government had found it easier to print money than to induce the peasantry to part with their rice at rates below the market price.

The misery of the many has in no way checked the squandermania of the few. President Sukarno's visits to foreign countries – accompanied by a large number of Ministers, advisers, pressmen, etc. – have become so frequent as barely to raise a smile. Some of these trips, it is true, are on genuine official business, as to the Cairo Non-Aligned Conference of 1964; even then, one may ask why Indonesia had to send the largest delegation. The usual purpose, however, is simply 'representation' or, in plain words, junketing. In return, foreign dignitaries have been entertained on a lavish scale in Indonesia, with Djakarta's badly fed crowds providing a well-drilled 'spontaneous' welcome.

The greatest failure of the régime, however, from the Indonesian point of view was in its inability to unite the country, as the very opposition to Malaysia bore witness. Nasution, the Defence Minister, and Subandrio, the Foreign Minister, have admitted that neither Malaysia nor the British bases there were a real threat to Indonesia. That the latter asserted that Malaysia could be used by outside powers to subvert and encircle Indonesia (with ten times the population of its neighbour) show the desperation of the faction. The truth seems more that the need for animosity exists only because Malaysia is an example of democracy, of economic progress and, surprisingly in view of its ethnic composition, of national conciliation. These are the very features Indonesia lacks. As such, it holds a dangerous appeal for the non-Javanese peoples of Indonesia, especially those of Sumatra, who have more cultural and historical links with the Malays than they have with the Javanese. If the Malays within Indonesia are to be kept cowed, those outside must be brought to acknowledge the supremacy of a Javanese-dominated Indonesia. The creation of an external enemy always has the attraction that those who oppose the government can be branded as traitors. This becomes irresistible when the external enemy, as is the case with Malaysia, is kin to those who are likely to oppose the government.

The faction had adopted the course of creating one enemy after another in an attempt to unite the country. But there were signs that the course was leading to disaster. They had lost the support, both political and material, of most of the Western world while the Soviet Union had shown that it was not prepared to back the régime to anything like the extent it had when the enemy had been the Netherlands in Western New Guinea. Even Afro-Asian opinion, despite its natural predilection to support anything calling itself anti-colonialism, had shown its condemnation of the hostilities against Malaysia and its dislike of the strident anti-Westernism advocated by Sukarno. For material support Indonesia was now compelled to rely largely on its two former enemies, the Netherlands and Japan; for political backing on communist China and those countries which supported her, such as North Vietnam and North Korea. It must be doubted if, on balance, Indonesia's foreign policy had gained more than it lost for the country.

Yet the Western world is not without blame in the matter. In the history both of Indonesian nationalism before independence, and of the state since, the 'moderates' achieved little success in obtaining satisfaction of their demands, whether it was greater representation in the Netherlands Indies, or their right to independence, or the incorporation of Western New Guinea into the Republic. The Dutch earlier, the Western world later, thus provided weapons for the Javanese extremist faction, who could reasonably argue that only their intransigent methods had brought, and would bring, satisfaction of Indonesian demands.

The foreign policy of the Javanese faction was one they learned in their revolutionary struggle against the Dutch. They then discovered that they were unlikely to obtain the help of a major power unless it was convinced that another would move in otherwise. Thus, in 1949 the United States applied its weight in favour of Indonesian independence only when it began to fear that a protracted conflict would lead to a communist take-over. Accordingly, when the faction determined to obtain Western New Guinea it courted the Soviet Union. The West, especially the United States, was told that the risks of Indonesia falling into the communist orbit were great if the territory were denied her. The size of the PKI, which had been encouraged to grow for domestic political reasons, lent some colour to this threat. Accordingly, the United States applied the necessary pressure, and the Indonesian flag flew over Western New Guinea.

Unfortunately, these circumstances had taught the Javanese faction only forms of rule which were appropriate to a people facing an external opponent, when internal conflicts could be left in abeyance.

After the incorporation of Western New Guinea, it was clear that a reconciliation of interests would have greatly modified the Javanese faction's dominant position. This, naturally enough, it was not prepared to accept. Instead, it drummed up opposition to Malaysia. The similarity of the method used to that of the campaign against the Dutch retention of Western New Guinea is obvious enough. Small-scale military actions, mob riots in Djakarta, expropriation of Malaysian and British property and its distribution to the faction's supporters, repeat the rituals of former years.

However, in early 1965 the world does not appear to have succumbed to the Javanese faction's pressure tactics; if anything the opposition to them is mounting. But it must be doubted if the faction is in a position to moderate its intransigence. Its position requires a permanent tension within the state, which enables the faction to tighten its military hold over other Indonesians, and the communists to consolidate their position among the Javanese. For these purposes xenophobia is indispensable.

78 A view of present-day Djakarta symbolizes modern Indonesia; the great Western-influenced status symbol of the Hotel Indonesia contrasted with the squalor of the near-by slum conditions.

79 Anti-Dutch feeling came to a head in 1957 when rioters burnt a mock dummy dressed in the flag of the Netherlands.

80 Indonesia was determined on driving the Dutch out. Here Netherlands nationals apply for exit visas.

81 In 1958 civil war broke out
between the Javanese government of Sukarno and the non-
Javanese faction. Refugees
escorted by troops of Minahasa
during this period.

82 Lieut.-Colonel Achmed
Hussein was head of the
Indonesian Revolutionary
Council which tried to topple
Sukarno but eventually failed.
This is one of many rallies held
at Batu Sankar in Central
Sumatra.

83 (*left*) In 1955 Indonesia acted as host to the Afro-Asian Conference at Bandung, Java. President Sukarno delivered the opening speech.

84 (*centre*) Indonesia was much opposed to the forming of Malaysia in July 1963. The US Attorney-General, Robert F. Kennedy, met Sukarno in January 1964 in an attempt to solve the crisis which ensued.

85 (*below*) This paved the way for a Summit Meeting at Tokyo in August 1964 at which Malaysia's Prime Minister, Tunku Abdul Rahman (third right) tried to solve his differences with Sukarno (second left); but the attempts failed.

86 Strong anti-British, anti-Malaysia riots broke out in Djakarta soon after the Federation had been formed.

87 Sukarno's plan in 1960 was the incorporation of Western New Guinea into the Republic. A typical Papuan (as the people of this island are called) family at Sorong.

88 Sukarno resorted to aggressiveness and Soviet aid in order to achieve his aim. Posters expressed Indonesian eventual victory.

89 An anti-SEATO demonstration at Djakarta in 1958.

90 Although slight tension arose between China and Indonesia in 1959 over the nationality of Chinese in Indonesia, this was finally resolved. Sukarno was given a great welcome on a visit to Peking in 1961.

91 By 1965 a solution to the armed 'confrontation' between Malaysia and Indonesia had not been reached. These infiltrators, picked up on Malaya's west coast, were part of a band of 24 guerrillas armed for destruction.

92 In January 1965 Indonesia resigned from the UN as a final protest against Malaysia. Sukarno encouraged anti-Malaysia and anti-Imperialist demonstrations such as this one.

Notes on the Text

3 EUROPEAN CONTENDERS
1 Colenbrander, H. T., *Jan Pieterszoon Coen. Beschieden omtrent zijn bedrijf in Indie*, 7 vols., The Hague, 1919–53, vol. 6, p. 156

5 THE AUTOCRATS
2 Dekker, E. Douwes ('Multatuli'), *Max Havelaar of de koffieveilingen der Nederlandsche Handelmaatschappij*, Amsterdam, Nederlandsche Bibliotheek, 1917. First edition appeared in 1860

7 GROWTH OF NATIONALISM
3 A Javanese title of nobility
4 *Sutan* or *Soetan* (abbreviated to *St.*) is a title of nobility among the Menang-kabau people of Sumatra

8 ACHIEVEMENT OF INDEPENDENCE
5 Mook, H. J. van, *Indonesië, Nederland en de Wereld*, Amsterdam, De Bezige Bij, 1949, p. 42
6 Kahin, G. McT., *Major Governments in Asia*, 2nd ed., Ithaca, N.Y., p. 585

10 THE ECONOMY
7 Humphrey, D. D., et al., *Indonesia: Perspective and Proposals for United States Economic Aid*, New Haven, Yale University, Southeast Asia Studies, 1963, pp. 90, 91
8 Ibid., pp. 43, 44
9 Economist Intelligence Unit, London. *Quarterly Economic Review – Indonesia*, April 1964, p. 5
10 Ibid., August 1964, pp. 2, 3

11 Hill, A. H., 'The Hikayat Abdullah, an annotated translation', *Journal of the Royal Asiatic Society, Malayan Branch*, 28 (1955)
12 Lubis, M., *Twilight in Djakarta*, translated from the Indonesian by C. Holt, London, 1963

13 *New York Times*, 18 May 1956
14 *Harian Rakjat*, 6 December 1963
15 Economist Intelligence Unit, London. *Quarterly Economic Review – Indonesia*, October 1964, p. 3
16 *The Times* (London), 17 February 1964

List of Abbreviations

KMT	Kuo Min Tang (Refugee government in Taiwan)
KNI	Komite Nasional Indonesia (Indonesian Assembly)
KNIP	Komite Nasional Indonesia Pusat (Indonesian National Assembly)
KPM	Koninklijke Paketvaart Maatschappij (Royal Packet Steamship Company)
MIAI	Madjlisul Islamil a'laa Indonesia (Muslim Organization)
NU	Nahdatul Ulama (Muslim Scholars)
PKI	Partai Komunis Indonesia (Indonesian Communist Party)
PNI	Perserikatan Nasional Indonesia (Indonesian Nationalist Association), later Partai Nasional Indonesia (Indonesian National Party)
PSI	Partai Sosialis Indonesia (Indonesian Socialist Party)
PUTERA	Pusat Tenaga Ra'ayat (People's United Front)
SOBSI	Serikat Organisasi Buruh Seluruh Indonesia (Indonesia's Central Federation of Trade Unions)
UNCI	United Nations Commission for Indonesia
USI	United States of Indonesia

Select Bibliography

PRE-HISTORY

Heekeren, H. R. van, *The Stone Age of Indonesia; The Bronze–Iron Age in Indonesia*, The Hague, 1957 and 1958. Probably the best studies of their period

Stutterheim, W. F., *Studies in Indonesian Archaeology*, The Hague, 1956. A general outline of Indonesian pre-history and archaeology

HISTORY

Anderson, B. R. O'G., *Some Aspects of Indonesian Politics under Japanese Occupation: 1944–45*, Ithaca, N.Y., 1961. A brief but essential study

Aziz, M. A., *Japan's Colonialism and Indonesia*, The Hague, 1955. An account of Japanese occupation policies in Indonesia

Bastin, J., *The Native Policies of Sir Stamford Raffles*, London, 1957. Valuable analysis of Raffles's liberalism

Benda, J., *The Crescent and the Rising Sun*, The Hague, 1958. The classic study of the Indonesian Muslim community during the Japanese occupation.

Bousquet, G. H., *A French View of the Netherlands Indies*, trans. by P. E. Lilienthal. London and New York, 1940. A critical essay by a French expert on North African Islam

Burger, D. H., *Structural Changes in Javanese Society: the supra-village sphere*; *Structural Changes in Javanese Society: the village sphere*, Ithaca, N.Y., 1956 and 1957. Two most useful analyses of the evolution of Javanese society

Cator, W. L., *The Economic Position of the Chinese in the Netherlands Indies*, Chicago, 1936. A helpful survey

Day, C., *The Policy and Administration of the Dutch in Java*, New York, 1904. Study of Dutch policy which emphasizes its worse characteristics

Elsbree, W. H., *Japan's Role in Southeast Asian Nationalist Movements, 1940–45*, Cambridge, Mass., 1953. Account of Japan's role in stimulating nationalist causes during the Second World War

Emerson, R., *Malaysia: A Study in Indirect Rule*, New York, 1937. An analysis of colonial rule in Indonesia and Malaya

Hall, D. G. E., *A History of South East Asia*, 2nd edn., London and New York, 1963. Sections on Indonesia contain all that is known with any certainty about its history

Kahin, G. McT., *Nationalism and Revolution in Indonesia*, New York, 1952. The classic account of the Indonesian nationalist struggle against Dutch rule

Kat Angelino, A. D. A. de, *Colonial Policy*, 2 vols., The Hague, 1931. Important work, which argued for a cultural synthesis

Klerck, E. S. de, *History of the Netherlands East Indies*, 2 vols., Rotterdam, 1938. A history of the Dutch in the archipelago, somewhat from a military standpoint

Leur, J. C. van, *Indonesian Trade and Society*, The Hague and Bandung, 1955. Pioneering study of the forms of Indonesian trade before the arrival of the West

Money, J. W. B., *Java*, 2 vols., London, 1861. A favourable British view of the Cultivation System

Niel, R. van, *The Emergence of the Modern Indonesian Élite*, The Hague, 1960. Excellent account of the development of nationalist leadership

Purcell, V., *The Chinese in Southeast Asia*, London, 1951. Contains a good history of the Chinese in Indonesia to the end of Dutch rule

Raffles, T. S., *A History of Java*, 2 vols., London, 1817. Perhaps the first serious history and survey of Indonesian life

Schrieke, B., ed., *The Effect of Western Influence on Native Civilizations in the Malay Archipelago*, Batavia, 1929. Collection of important essays

Soedjatmoko, A. B., *An Approach to Indonesian History: Towards an Open Future*, New York, 1960. An argument against nationalist distortions of history, by a leading Indonesian publicist

Vandendosch, A., *The Dutch East Indies: Its Government, Problems, and Politics*, Berkeley and Los Angeles, 1942. An excellent account of Dutch colonial rule

Vlekke, B. H. M., *Nusantara: A History of Indonesia*, rev. edn., Chicago, 1960. General survey of the archipelago's history

Wehl, D., *The Birth of Indonesia*, London, 1948. Account of the 1945–7 period by, apparently, a member of the British forces

Wertheim, W. F., *Indonesian Society in Transition*, The Hague, 1956. A sociological, and somewhat Marxist, analysis of history

Williams, L. E., *Overseas Chinese Nationalism: The Genesis of the Pan-Chinese Movement in Indonesia, 1900–1916*, Illinois, 1960. A thorough study

Wolf, C., Jr., *The Indonesian Story*, New York, 1948. Covers the Dutch-Indonesian negotiations of the 1945–9 period

SOCIOLOGY

Geertz, C., *The Religion of Java*, Illinois, 1960. Excellent ethnographic account of Javanese religious beliefs and practices

Geertz, H., *The Javanese Family*, New York, 1961. A most valuable ethnographic study

Haar, B. Ter., *Adat Law in Indonesia*, New York, 1948. The classic summary of Indonesian customary law

Josselin de Jong, P. E. de, *Minangkabau and Negri Sembilan: Socio-political structure in Indonesia*, Leyden, 1951. A reconstruction and analysis of the 'ideal' Minangkabau society

Kroef, J. M. van der, *Indonesia in the Modern World*, 2 vols., Bandung, 1952 and 1954. Sociological essays on many subjects

Palmier, L. H., *Social Status and Power in Java*, London, 1960. Study of the *élites* of two Javanese towns

Schrieke, B., *Indonesian Sociological Studies*, Parts I and II; The Hague and Bandung, 1955 and 1957. A selection of sociological essays on a number of problems, past and present

Selosoemardjan, *Social Changes in Jogjakarta*, New York, 1962. An excellent account of the first decade of independence

Snouck, H. C., *The Achehnese*, 2 vols., Leyden, 1906. Classic study of the culture and social structure of Atjeh in 1901

Vreede-De Stuers, C., *The Indonesian Woman: Struggles and Achievements*, The Hague, 1960. Useful account of the changing position of the Indonesian upper middle-class woman

Wertheim, W. F., *et al.*, eds., *Bali: Studies in Life, Thought, and Ritual*, The Hague and Bandung, 1960. A selection of important studies of Balinese culture and religion, both pre-war and present day

Wertheim, W. F., *et al.*, eds., *The Indonesian Town: Studies in Urban Sociology*, The Hague and Bandung, 1958. Discussions of various aspects of urban development in Java up to 1938

Willmot, D. E., *The Chinese of Semarang: A Changing Minority Community in Indonesia*, New York, 1960. A very useful account

ECONOMICS

Boeke, J. H., *Economics and Economic Policy of Dual Societies*, New York, 1953. An analysis of the effect on economic behaviour of different cultural imperatives

Dewey, A. G., *Peasant Marketing in Java*, New York, 1962. An interesting account of a peasant market in East Java

Fryer, D. W., 'Economic Aspects of Indonesian Disunity', *Pacific Affairs*, xxx (Sept. 1957), pp. 195–208. An important article bringing out the basic conflict of economic interest between Javanese and other Indonesians

Geertz, C., *The Development of the Javanese Economy: A Socio-cultural Approach*, Cambridge, Mass., 1956. A study of the social consequences of the sugar industry in Java

Hatta, M., *The Co-operative Movement in Indonesia*, New York, 1957. A history of Indonesian co-operatives which also gives the ex-Vice-President's economic and political views

Humphrey, D. D., *et al.*, *Indonesia: Perspectives and Proposals for United States Economic Aid*, New Haven, 1963. Very good study of major aspects of the Indonesian economy

Paauw, D. S., *Financing Economic Development: The Indonesian Case*, Illinois, 1960. Excellent analysis of Indonesian economic problems

Soedjatmoko, A. B., *Economic Development as a Cultural Problem* (Cornell Modern Indonesian Project, Translation Series), New York, 1958. A brief but important argument

Sutter, J. O., *Indonesianisasi: Politics in a Changing Economy, 1940–1955* (Southeast Asia Programme, Cornell University, Data Paper No. 36), New York, 1959. A thorough review of the effect of Indonesian politics on the economy

Wertheim, W. F., *et al.*, eds., *Indonesian Economics*, The Hague, 1961. An interesting collection of essays debating the validity of a 'dual economy'

CONTEMPORARY ARTS

Ali, A., *The Flaming Earth: Poems from Indonesia*, Karachi, Friends of the Indonesian People Society, 1949. A selection from the best Indonesian poetry of the 1945–9 period

Belo, J., *Trance in Bali*, New York, 1960. Excellent description and analysis of this Balinese phenomenon

Bernet Kempers, A. J., *Ancient Indonesian Art*, Amsterdam, 1959. Illustrated and reliable survey of Java's ancient plastic arts by an archaeologist

Kunst, J., *Music in Java, its History, its Theory and its Technique*, 2 vols., The Hague, 1949. The classic account

Echols, J. M., *Indonesian Writing in Translation*, New York, 1956. A very good sample of Indonesian work

Mangkunegara VII of Surakata, K.G.P.A.A., *On the Wajang Kulit (Purwa) and its Symbolic and Mystical Elements*, New York, 1957. An examination of the mystical and philosophical implications of the shadow play

McPhee, C., *Music of Bali*, Yale, 1963. Excellent description, a counterpart to Kunst's *Music in Java*

Wagner, F. A., *Indonesia*, London, 1959. Perhaps the most useful general account of the Indonesian arts

Zoete, B. de and Walter Spies, *Dance and Drama in Bali*, New York, 1939. The best introduction to its subject

CONTEMPORARY AFFAIRS

Feith, H., *The Decline of Constitutional Democracy in Indonesia*, Ithaca, N.Y., 1962. Excellent study of Indonesian politics from 1949 to 1957

Fischer, L., *The Study of Indonesia*, New York, 1959. Valuable for its inter-views with Sukarno

Hanna, W. A., *Bung Karno's Indonesia*, New York, 1961. A series of first-hand reports of Indonesian conditions in 1959

Hatta, M., *Past and Future* (Cornell Modern Indonesia Project, Translation Series). New York, 1960. Sets out the ex-Vice-President's political philosophy

Kahin, G. McT., ed., *Major Governments of Asia*, 2nd edn., New York, 1963. Section on 'Indonesia' by the editor. An excellent account of contemporary politics by an author noted for his sympathy with Indonesian nationalism

Legge, J. D., *Central Authority and Regional Autonomy in Indonesia: A Study in Local Administration, 1950–1960*, New York, 1961. Thorough analysis of changes in the period

McVey, R., ed., *Indonesia*, New Haven, 1963. A very good collection of articles covering the most important aspects of the Indonesian scene

Netherlands Ministry of Foreign Affairs. *Administration of Justice in Indonesia: an account of the treatment of Netherlands prisoners and Defence Counsel in Indonesia, 1953–1955*, The Hague, 1955. Refers to the political trials of the period

Palmier, L. H., *Indonesia and the Dutch*, London, 1962. Analysis of internal stresses in Indonesia and their effects on government policy

Reed, S. W., ed., *Indonesia*, 3 vols., New Haven, 1956. An earlier compilation than McVey's but still of use

Sjahrir, S., *Out of Exile*, New York, 1949. A description of conditions in the 1930s by the socialist leader, now detained without trial

Soedjatmoko, A. B., 'The Role of Political Parties in Indonesia', in P. W. Thayer, ed., *Nationalism and Progress in Free Asia*, Baltimore, 1956, pp. 128–40. Focuses on the 1955 elections

Taylor, A. M., *Indonesian Independence and the United Nations*, London, 1960. Account of the part played by the U N in bringing about Indonesian independence

Who's Who

ABDULGANI, Ruslan, b. 1914. Attended a Training College for Teachers, but was expelled when he became Chairman of the Pergerakan Indonesia Muda (Young Indonesia Movement). He led Sjahrir's younger followers in the underground movement during the Second World War. He was simultaneously head of the Surabaya branch of a Japanese-sponsored youth organization, the Angkatan Muda, in 1944, and Chairman of the East Java Information Committee of the local revolutionary KNI. In 1951 he was a member of the Indonesian delegation to the UN General Assembly at Paris. Became Foreign Minister in 1956. Arrested by the Army for questioning on corruption charges, he was released by the intervention of Prime Minister Ali Sastroamidjojo on the eve of the Suez Conference in London in 1956. Appointed Deputy Chairman of the National Council on its formation in 1957, he became Chairman of its successor, the Supreme Advisory Council in 1959, and Minister-Coordinator of People's Relations in 1963.

AIDIT, Dipa Nusantara, b. 1921. Secretary-General of the PKI. Joined the Persatuan Indonesia Timur (East Indonesia Organization) in 1939 and the Gerindo Indonesian People's Movement in 1940. During the Japanese occupation was active in the Persatuan Buruh Kendaraan (Vehicle Workers' Union) and the (underground) PKI in 1943. Organized Gerakan Indonesia Merdeka, Gerindom (Movement for a Free Indonesia). After independence he was instrumental in founding the Angkatan Pemuda Indonesia (Indonesian Youth Organization), and was active in the Barisan Buruh Indonesia (Indonesian Workers' Corps), which later was to grow into the SOBSI. Elected a member of the Central Committee of the PKI in 1947, and a year later became a member of the Politburo. In 1951 he became Secretary-General of the PKI. Visited Moscow in 1956 as head of the Indonesian communist delegation to the Twentieth Congress of the Communist Party. He was appointed Vice-Chairman of the Provisional People's Consultative Congress with the rank of Minister in 1962. In addition to being Secretary-General of the PKI, Aidit also heads the party's Politburo and its Central Committee.

225

BOSCH, Johannes Van den (1780–1844). Probably the greatest colonial states-man of the Netherlands after Coen. He joined the Netherlands army as a boy and went to the East Indies. As a result of a dispute Daendels deported him in 1810. King William I of Holland sent him in 1827 to the West Indies to study their economy. He returned the next year with a plan on how to make the islands profitable. The king was so impressed that Van den Bosch was appointed Governor-General of the East Indies. Introduced the Cultuurstelsel (Forced Cultivation System) in Java which turned Java's deficits into surpluses and replenished the Netherlands' depleted reserves.

COEN, Jan Pieterszoon (1587–1629). Founder of the Dutch Empire in the East. In 1618 he was appointed Governor-General of the Dutch East Indies. He died in 1629 at Batavia, the city he had founded, on the eve of the defeat of the Mataram army which had been investing the city. During his service in the East he chased the English out of Indonesian waters, and so ensured Dutch dominion; by ruthless methods he secured a monopoly of the spice trade for the Company; and he also shifted the base of its operations from spices for Europe to trade in Asia.

DAENDELS, Herman Willem (1762–1818). Began his career as a lawyer. In 1807 he was appointed Governor-General of the Indies, and charged with reorganizing the administration and strengthening the military defences of Java in the French interest. He achieved his aim, thus indirectly preparing the ground for Raffles, but the means he employed led to so much discontent that in 1810 he was recalled by Napoleon, who had just annexed the Netherlands to his empire.

DIPONEGORO, Prince (1785–1855). Regarded in Indonesia as the progenitor of nationalism. He was born the eldest son of the Sultan of Jogyakarta. He grew into a religious fanatic, spending much time in solitary meditation in sacred caves, and acquired very great influence. During the British occupation (1811–16), Javanese *adat* law compelled his being passed over in the succession to the throne in favour of a younger brother. Raffles, the Governor-General, then promised him that he would be next in line of succession. The brother died in 1822 but the Dutch, who once again were ruling Java, being ignorant of Raffles's promise, gave the succession to the dead Sultan's two-year-old son. As a result of further quarrels with the Dutch, Diponegoro raised a revolt and the common people flocked to him as Allah's chosen instrument to drive out the unbelievers. The struggle lasted until 1829 when the Dutch achieved mastery. The next year Diponegoro himself offered to negotiate, but at the resulting conference refused to give up the title of Sultan and Protector of Islam in Java. He was thereupon arrested and banished to the Celebes, where he died in 1855.

HATTA, Mohammed, b. 1902. Vice-President (1945-56). Educated at the Secondary School in Padang. Read Economics at Rotterdam University. While there he helped found the Perhimpunan Indonesia (Indonesian Association). In 1927 he was arrested in the Netherlands and tried for inciting revolution, but the case was dismissed for lack of evidence. In 1932 he became Chairman of the Club Pendidikan Nasional Indonesia (Indonesian National Education Club), with Sjahrir as his chief lieutenant. They were arrested together and exiled in 1934 until 1942. On release he became Vice-President of the PUTERA. He was also active in the Djawa Hokokai (People's Loyalty Organization of Java). Appointed Vice-President of the Indonesian Republic in 1945. Assumed the office of Prime Minister in addition in 1948; in December of that year he was captured by the Dutch and confined on Bangka Island. He was returned (with Sukarno and other leaders) to Jogyakarta in July 1949, and resumed his offices of Vice-President and Prime Minister. He led the Republican delegation to the Round Table Conference at The Hague and initialled the draft provisional constitution of the United States of Indonesia, 29 October 1949. Elected Vice-President of the unitarian Republic of Indonesia in 1950-6. Being unable to agree on national policy with Sukarno he resigned and retired into private life in 1956.

KARTAWIDJAJA, Djuanda (1911-63). The Prime Minister of 'Guided Democracy'. He was appointed an engineer in the West Java Provincial Government Department of Works in 1937, and in 1942 he became a member of the Regents' Council of Batavia. Chairman of the financial commission of the Indonesian delegation which negotiated the transfer of sovereignty at The Hague in 1949. Became Prime Minister in the era of 'Guided Democracy' from 1957 to his death in 1963 when the post was abolished.

KARTINI, *Raden Adjeng* (1879-1904). She marks the beginning of modern Indonesian nationalism. In order to diffuse Western education among girls, Kartini opened a small school in her father's (Regent of Japara) house in 1903. She died at the age of twenty-five. Her letters to Dutch correspondents, published after her death, evoked great enthusiasm for nationalism among young Indonesians, and roused sympathy abroad for Indonesian feminism.

LEIMENA, Johannes, b. 1905. Second Deputy Prime Minister. Qualified doctor. At the time of the Japanese invasion he was head of a mission hospital in Central Java. After six months' imprisonment by the Japanese, he took up his profession again in Central Java. On independence, he became a member of the KNI at Tanggerang in Central Java. In 1946 he joined the KNIP as a representative of the Indonesian Christian Party. He held portfolios of public health in several Republican cabinets between 1945 and 1949. A member of committees charged with negotiating with the Dutch, and of the Republican delegation to the Round Table Conference at The Hague in 1949. Became Minister of Health in several cabinets after the transfer of sovereignty, including those established under the system of 'Guided Democracy', and in 1963 was appointed to his present position.

LUBIS, Zulkifli, b. 1924. Appointed Deputy Chief of Staff of the Army in 1953 as a result of siding with Sukarno over the 17 October affair. He attempted to foment a military coup in 1956 but failed. On 30 November 1957 a group of his young followers attempted to assassinate President Sukarno; their failure set off the chain of events which began with the eviction of the Dutch from Indonesia, continued with the crushing of the movements for local self-government and ended with the imposition of 'Guided Democracy'. Lubis finally gave himself up in September 1961 in response to a government offer of amnesty.

MOOK, H. J. van, b. 1894. A member of the De Stuw (Forward Movement) group of Dutch progressives in the pre-war Netherlands Indies. Evacuated from the Indies when the Japanese attacked, he was later sent to Australia in 1944 with powers to assume charge of the administration when the war ended, and to set up a provisional Netherlands Indies government. He was appointed Lieutenant Governor-General in 1945 (no Governor-General was appointed after the Second World War), but lost this position in July 1948 as a result of a change of government in the Netherlands. Though willing to come to terms with Indonesian nationalism, he had received inadequate support from the government at The Hague.

NASUTION, General Abdul Haris, b. 1918. Minister of Defence. Commissioned in the KNIL (Royal Netherlands Indies Army) in 1941. During the Japanese occupation, he worked in the civil administration. After independence he became Chief of Staff, Commando I, Bandung Division, Commander of Division I, Purwakarta and in 1946 Deputy Supreme Commander, Jogyakarta. Appointed Chief of Staff of the Army in 1952, but was suspended from his post after organizing a demonstration in favour of the dissolution of the provisional parliament and the holding of general elections (17 October affair) in 1952.

Reputedly the author of the government decision to use force against the rebels of 1958. He is also thought to be responsible for the plan, adopted in 1959 by President Sukarno, to reinstate the 1945 Constitution providing for a Presidential cabinet, in which he was appointed Minister of Defence in 1959. In 1962 Sukarno deprived him of direct control over troops by promoting him Chief of Staff of the Combined Armed Services; while leaving him Defence Minister. A cabinet reshuffle in 1963 carried the process further by down-grading his position in that body.

NATSIR, Mohammed, b. 1908. A leader of the moderate left wing of the Masjumi (Modernist Muslim) Party. In 1940 he became Chairman of the Bandung Branch of the Partai Islam Indonesia; he was also a member of other Muslim organizations. He was Minister of Information 1945–7, 1948–9. Elected to the governing body of the Masjumi in 1948. In 1949 he was chosen President of the Masjumi Party Assembly and appointed Masjumi member of the Provisional Parliament of the United States of Indonesia. He was Prime Minister of the first cabinet of the Unitary Republic in 1950. Compelled to resign in March 1951 when his policy of negotiating with the Dutch over Western New Guinea failed. The next ministry was headed by Sukiman, a conservative leader of the Masjumi, and Natsir lost his influence in the Masjumi councils. He attempted to set up an alternative government in 1958 and was placed under detention in 1961.

RAFFLES, Thomas Stamford (1781–1826). At the age of fourteen he entered the service of the British East India Company's office in London as a clerk. In 1810 he was appointed 'Agent to the Governor-General with the Malay States', and in the following year Lieutenant Governor-General of Java.

During his term of office, Raffles, building on the foundations laid by Daen-dels, reduced the powers of the local rulers and made many administrative changes, based on British-Indian methods. He also reformed the administration of justice, abolishing torture in all legal processes. However, Raffles failed to make Java pay, and early in 1815 he was removed from office and returned home. He founded Singapore in 1819.

SASTROAMIDJOJO, Ali, b. 1903. Read law at Leyden University and was detained by the Netherlands government for six months for activity as a member of the Perhimpunan Indonesia in 1927. In 1928 he returned to Indonesia to practise law and to edit *Djanget*. He joined Sukarno's PNI and edited the party's organ *Suluh Indonesia Muda* in 1928-9. Chairman of the Madiun branch of the Gerindo 1939-41. Deputy Minister of Information in the Sukarno cabinet, August to November 1945, and in 1947 attended the Asian Relations Conference at New Delhi. He was appointed Minister of Education in the Sjarifuddin cabinet, 27 June 1947 to 27 January 1948; and in the 1st Hatta cabinet 29 January 1948 to 27 December 1949. Exiled with Sukarno and others 1948-9. Member of the Republican delegation to the Round Table Conference at The Hague in 1949. Prime Minister 1953-5, 1956-7; his cabinet was notorious for corruption. It fell in the face of revolts among the non-Javanese.

SJAHRIR, *Sutan*, b. 1909. Socialist leader. Read law at Leyden University and was active in the Perhimpunan Indonesia. Chairman of the Golongon Merdeka (Independence Group) in 1931 which became the Club Pendidikan Nasional Indonesia (Indonesian National Education Club) in the next year. In 1934, he was arrested with Mohammed Hatta, and both were exiled from 1934-42 by the Dutch. In 1945 he organized revolts among underground workers and students against the Japanese, which forced Sukarno to proclaim independence. He was author of *Perdjuangan Kita* (Our Struggle), published in 1945, which had much influence on Indonesian revolutionary thought. He was elected Chairman, 1st KNIP Working Committee in October 1945; and headed the new PSI early in December 1945. Prime Minister 1945-7. Exiled by the Dutch with Sukarno and Hatta in 1948. His party was proscribed by Sukarno in 1961, and he was jailed without trial in 1963.

SUBANDRIO, Dr., b. 1915. Foreign Minister and First Deputy Prime Minister. Trained in medicine and practised surgery for three years. After independence appointed Secretary-General of the Ministry of Information. In 1947 he was sent to London as Republican representative, and when sovereignty was transferred in 1949 he became Indonesia's first ambassador to London. In 1954 he was appointed ambassador to Moscow, but returned to Indonesia in 1956 to become Secretary-General at the Ministry of Foreign Affairs. The next year he became Foreign Minister, a post he has held ever since. In 1963 he was concurrently appointed First Deputy Prime Minister.

SUKARNO, President of Indonesia, b. 1901 at Blitar, in East Java. His father, an elementary school teacher, came from that region, but his mother was Balinese. He completed his education at the Bandung Technical College, graduating as an engineer. Entered politics in 1926. Organized the Bandung Study Club which became the nucleus of the Perserikatan Nasional Indonesia (Indonesian Nationalist Association) in 1927 (later Partai Nasional Indonesia) on the principle of non-co-operation with the Dutch colonial authorities. Arrested by the Dutch in 1929, tried in 1930, and imprisoned until 1932. Joined the Partai Indonesia or Partindo (Indonesian Party), and was made its Chairman. Again summarily arrested in 1933 he was exiled without trial to the island of Flores, later transferred to Benkulen, and released only by the Japanese in 1942. They appointed him Chairman of their nationalist organization, the PUTERA, in 1943 and later President of a consultative appointed council to represent Indonesia, the Djawa Hokokai (People's Loyalty Organization of Java).

In June 1945, Sukarno outlined the Five Principles, or *Pantja Sila* (nationalism, humanitarianism, representative government, social justice, and belief in God) which were to become the mottoes of the Indonesian state. In August 1945 he was elected President of the Indonesian Republic, a position he has held ever since. In December 1948 he was captured by the Dutch, and was returned to Jogyakarta in July 1949. Elected President of the United States of Indonesia in the same year. During 1950, faced with a revolt in the South Moluccas against the dissolution of the Federation, he used force to suppress it. In 1952 he withstood an Army demand that he dissolve Parliament (the 17 October affair). This did not indicate his satisfaction with the functioning of parliamentary democracy. After a visit in 1956 to the United States, the Soviet Union, and communist China, during which he had been most impressed by the last, he called for the abandonment of parliamentary democracy, the dissolution of the political parties, and the institution of a system of 'Guided Democracy'. This precipitated an attempt, based in Sumatra and Celebes, to set up an alternative government, and Sukarno ordered the Army to eliminate the dissidents. In 1959 he dismissed the elected Constituent Assembly and imposed the 1945 Constitution, which enshrined a presidential cabinet. Increasingly he concentrated his energies on a campaign to incorporate Western New Guinea into the Republic, and achieved his aim in late 1962. He thereupon turned to oppose the formation of the Federation of Malaysia. In 1963, in a cabinet reshuffle, he abolished the independent position of Prime Minister and assumed it himself. Since 1956 he has made frequent visits to other countries both to obtain support for his policies and for recreation.

SUKIMAN, Wirjosandjojo, b. 1896. Trained as a doctor. Chairman of the Perhimpunan Indonesia (Indonesian Association) in 1925. During the

Japanese occupation he was prominent in the MIAI, and was Vice-Chairman of the PUTERA. When the struggle for independence began in 1945, he became a member of the KNIP and of the Supreme Advisory Council. He was also appointed chairman of the Masjumi. In Hatta's first cabinet, in 1948, Sukiman became Minister of Internal Affairs, but joined the guerrillas during the Dutch second military action. In the sovereign Indonesian state he was appointed Prime Minister from 27 April 1951 to 23 February 1952. During his period of office relations with the West were improved, and a large number of subversive elements, mostly left-wing, were detained. He also nationalized the Java Bank, Indonesia's principal issue house, and expropriated foreign-owned lands.

Acknowledgements

Associated Press, 45, 57, 58, 59, 82, 86; from Sir J. Brooke, *Borneo and the Celebes*, 1848, by courtesy of the Trustees of the British Museum, 26; Camera Press, 1, 6, 52, 61, 63, 70, 77, 79, 83, 90 (John Bulmer), 78, 88, 91, 92; by courtesy of the Embassy of the Republic of Indonesia, 3, 4, 16, 30, 38, 40, 46, 48, 50, 55, 60, 62, 65, 66, 69, 71, 72, 73, 81; from G. de Eredia, *Malaca, l'Inde Méridionale et le Cathay*, 1613 (edition of 1882), by courtesy of the Trustees of the British Museum, 19; Keystone Press Agency, 7, 18, 47, 51, 67, 80, 84, 85, 87, 89; by courtesy of Koninklijk Instituut Voor de Tropen, 15, 17, 20, 21, 23, 27, 29, 33, 34, 35, 37, 42, 43, 44, 49; by courtesy of the New York Public Library, 8; Pictorial Press, 39; from T. S. Raffles, *History of Java*, 1817, by courtesy of the Trustees of the British Museum, 10, 36; Radio Times Hulton Picture Library, 22, 24, 25, 32, 41; by courtesy of Rijksinstituut voor Oorlogdocumentatie, 53, 54, 56; by courtesy of the Rijksmuseum Amsterdam, 11, 13; J. Sheerboom, 9; W. Suschitzky, 2, 5, 12, 14, 28, 31, 64, 68, 74, 75, 76.

Index

233

Brahma, 18, 20, *11*
Brahmanism, 15, 16, 18, 20
Brahmins, 15, 16
Britain, 101, 108, 204
British, the, 39, 41, 42, 43, 44, 45, 48, 51, 61, 64, 65, 69, 75, 107-8, 137, 201, *25*
British East India Company, 62-3
Brooke, James, 75
Brunei, 199, *26*; Prince of, 38
Bubonic plague, 78
Buddhism, 15-17, 21, 127 (*see also* Hinayana and Mahayana)
Buddhist art, 17
Budi Utomo (High Endeavour), 91, 92
Bunker, Ellsworth, 199
Burma, 78

CAIRO NON-ALIGNED CONFERENCE, 203, 206
Canals, 45
Capellen, Van der, 65
Cassava, 71, 139, 150, 151
Cattle rearing, 139
Cavendish, 38
Celebes (Sulawesi), 10, 11, 12, 39, 41, 66, 108, 167, 185, 187, 190, 193, 205
Census 1961 and 1930, 11
Central Advisory Board, 105
Central Bureau of Statistics, the, 156
Central Java, 10, 11, 19, 20, 65, 124, 128, 129, 131, 167, 170, 175, 181
Central Sumatra, 11, 100, 135, 138, 181, 190, 192, 193
Ceylon, 42, 50
Chamber of the Peoples' Representative, the, 104
Chemical industry, 145
Cheribon, 51, 63
China, 9, 15, 17, 21, 26, 42, 45, 71, 133, 144, 190, 195, 207
China Sea, 21
Chinese, the, 49, 50, 63, 65, 67, 69, 70, 80, 90, 91, 96, 100, 101, 141, 179, 195, 196, 201, 202, 203, *17*
Chinese Peoples' Republic, 195
Chola (Indian ruler), 20

Christian communities, 126
Cinchona, 71
Cinnamon, 71
Civil Service, the, 80, 91; European, 96; Indonesian, 96, 106, 122, 195
Clerkship Examination, 80
Climate, 12
Clothing, production of, 148
Clove trade, 38
Coal, 142, 154, *70*
Coastal Malay, 11
Coconut palms, 13
Coen, J. P. (*see* Who's Who: p. 226), 40-1, 42, 112, *24*
Coffee, 13, 46-8, 62, 68, 69, 71, 73, 74, 140, 141, 152, *30*
Colombo Plan, 204
Commissioner for Native Affairs, 48
Communism, 97, 98; *see also* PKI
Communists, 186, 187, 190, 191, 208
Concentration camps, 105
Conservatives, the, 71
Copper, 42, 142
Copra, 140, 149, 152, 153, 187, *68*
Coromandel (Cholamandala), coast of, 15, 20, 21, *21*
Council of the Indies, the, 104
Covarrubias, Miguel, 177
Cultivation, 13, 74; shifting of, 138; primitive methods of, 138; and food crops, 139; and cash crops, 140
Cultuurstelsel (Forced Cultivation System), 67-9, 74, 77
Czechoslovakia, 194

DAENDELS, H. W. (*see* Who's Who: p. 226), 61-2, 63, 64, 65, 67, 68, *33*
Dalang, the, 170, 171, 175, 176
Dance, 166, 169, 175-6, *74*
Danes, the, 39, 43, 44, 45
Darul Islam, 184, 185, 198
Decentralization Law (1903), 91
Dekker, Douwes, 71
Deli, 141
Demak, Principality of, 27, 39
Dewi Sri, 128
De Stuw (Forward Movement), 102

Dhyani Buddhas, 17, 19
Diemen, A. Van, 42
Dieng plateau (temples on), 19, *10*
Diponegoro, Prince (*see* Who's Who: p. 226), 65–6, 185, *34*
Divorce, 133–4
Djakarta, 12, 112, 124, 145, 156, 178, 195, 198, 200, 205, 206, *28*, *78* (*see also* Batavia)
Djawa Kuno (ancient Javanese language), 167
Drake, Francis, 38, *20*
Drama, 166, 169, 176
Dry-field crops, 139
Durga, 128
Dutch, the, 13, 38–41, 42, 43, 46, 49–50, 62, 64, 65, 66, 67, 68, 70, 75, 76, 79, 90, 95, 96, 98, 100, 101, 102, 103, 104, 105, 106, 107, 108, 109, 110, 112, 121, 122, 137, 166, 171, 178, 180, 182, 185, 191–2, 195, 196, 207, *79*, *80*
Dutch language, 95, 121
Dutch East India Company, *see* United East India Company
Dutch Gold Coast, 75

EAST INDONESIA, 109, 169, 192
East Java, 11, 19, 20, 131, 139, 141, 167, 181, 183, 184
Economy, the, 90, 137–56; aims, 137–8; food crops, 138–9; cash crops, 140–1, 151–3, 187; industrialization, 141–3; and foreign aid, 144–8; and the Plan, 146–9; and food, 150–1; and minerals, 154; and revenue and expenditure, 155–6
Education, 75, 78–80, 92, 98, 99–100, 106, 122, 123, 182, *62*, *63*
Egypt, 168, 194
Eight-Year Development Plan (1961–9), 148, *66*
English language, the, 121
Equator, the, 12
'Ethical Policy', 77, 79, 89
Ethnic groups, 69, 96, 97, 131–6, 166, 169, 180, 182

Eurasians, 92, 93, 96, 100, 101, 105, 141, 169, 192
Europe, 37, 40, 41, 49, 66, 67, 73, 77, 101
Europeans, 67, 69, 73, 74, 75, 76, 80, 90, 91, 92, 93, 94, 96, 101, 102, 105, 166

FEDERALISTS, THE, 111, 112
Feminism, 134
Film industry, 176
First National Congress (1916), 93
'First Police Action', 109
First World War, 99
Fishing, 14, *6*
Forced Cultivation System, *see* Cultuurstelsel
Foreign aid, 144–8, 205
'Foreign Asians', 69
'Foreign Orientals', 96
France, 51
Franco-British-American War (1780), 51
French, the, 44, 51, 67, 69
French Revolution, the, 51, 63
Fundamental Law of the Netherlands (1922), 95, 97

GAMA, VASCO DA, 37
Gamelan orchestra, 169–70, 172, 175, 77
Gautama, Siddharta (the Buddha), 16
Geography, 12
Gide, André, 168
Goa, 37
Gold Standard, the, 101
Good Offices Committee (GOC), 109, 110
Gotong royong (mutual aid), 132
Graphic arts, 166, 176–7
Great depression, the (1929), 78, 90, 98, 100, 101, 137
'Guided Democracy', 190, 193, 195, 205
Gujaratis, the, 21, 27

HADITH (TRADITION), THE, 92, 129, 131
Hadj, the (pilgrimage to Mecca), 130
Hague, The, 77

Hague Agreement, the, 187
Hatta, Mohammed (*see* Who's Who: p. 227), 103, 107, 110, 181, 184, 190, 191, 193, 199, *56*
Hemingway, Ernest, 168
Heutsz, Van, 77
Hinayana (Lesser Vehicle), 17
Hindu Brahmins, 15
Hinduism, 15–16, 18, 21, 128, 130; influence on culture, 168, 174, 176, 177
House of Representatives, the, 111
Hurgronje, Snouck, 76
Hydro-electric power, 142

IKAT CLOTH, 178
India, 14, 15, 17, 18, 21, 25, 28, 42, 47, 109, 128, 133, 194; influence on culture, 169, 173
Indian Muslims, 179
Indians, 69
Independence Preparatory Committee, 107
Indies Social Democratic Association, 94
Indies Society, the, 92, 96
Indigo, 67
Indo-China, 9
Indonesian Army, 106, 183, 190, 193, 197, 198, 201
Indonesian culture, an, 166, 168
Indonesian language, 10, 168
Industrialization, 99
Inflation, 151
Investment, 143
Iron, 142, 145
Irrawaddy delta, 78
Islam, 21, 26–7, 37, 39, 44, 45, 92, 93, 126, 127–31, 133, 135, 136, 168, 169, 171, 172, 174, 175, 177, 180, 185, 197 (*see also* orthodox Islam and modernist Islam)
Islam statistik (Muslims for statistical purposes), 130
Islamic state of Indonesia, 184, 185
Italy, 75

JAINISM, 16
Jakatra, 41

Jambi, 18
Japan, 17, 21, 41, 42, 101, 104, 144, 207
Japanese, the, 100, 104; invasion of, 76, 104, 105, *53*; occupation of, 105–7, 166, 168, 177, 178, 184, 192, *54*, *55*
Java, 9, 10, 11, 12, 13, 17, 19, 20, 21, 25, 26, 39, 41, 44, 47, 49, 50, 51, 61, 62, 63, 66, 68, 70, 71, 75, 76, 77, 78, 79, 89, 92, 108, 109, 110, 122, 124, 127, 128, 131, 134, 138, 139, 140, 142, 168, 169, 171, 173, 177, 178, 180, 184, 187, 193 (*see also* East Java, Central Java and West Java)
Javanese, 11, 66, 70, 76, 92, 128, 130, 131, 132, 133, 134, 135, 136, 165, 166, 175, 179, 180, 182, 183, 184, 206, 208, *1*, *35*
Javanese faction, the, 181, 183, 184, 185, 186, 187, 190, 191, 192–4, 195, 197, 204, 207, 208
Javanese language, 92, 123, 167
Java sea, 41, 175
Java War (1825–30), the, 65, 68, 71
Jogyakarta, 20, 50, 51, 63, 65, 66, 122, 170, 179; Sultan of, 65, 193
Johore, 39

KAIN (SKIRT), 134
Kalimantan, *see* Borneo
Kantjil (mouse-deer), the, 167
Karma, 16
Kartawidjaja, Djuanda, 191
Kennedy, Robert, 201, *84*
Khan, Kublai (Emperor of China), 21
KMT (Refugee government in Taiwan), 195
Komedi Stambul (type of drama), 176
Koran, the, 92, 129, 131
Korea, 104
KPM (Royal Packet Steamship Company), 192
Krontjong, the, 169
Kartini, *Raden Adjeng* (*see* Who's Who: p. 227), 90, 92
Kraton (capital), 25, 46, 172
Krishna, 18

LABUAN, 75
Lakons, the, 173
Land-holdings, 125
Land-taxes, 70
Language, 10
Lebaran (Islamic feast), 130
Lesser Sunda Islands, 11, 13, 15, 139
Liberal policy, 73–4
Liberals, the, 71, 72, 74, 75
Linggadjati Agreement, the, 109
Lisbon, Port of, 39
Literature, 166–8
Lombok, island of, 76, 128
Lubis, Mochtar, 169
Lubis, Z. (*see* Who's Who: p. 228), 187
Luzon, 10

MACAO, 40
Macapagal, President, 200, 201
Mada, Gadjak, 22, 25, 26
Madagascar, 9, 10
Madjapahit, Empire of, 22–6, 27, 129, 170, 171, 180
Madura, 11, 13, 40, 46, 66, 139
Madurese, 11
Magellan, 37
Mahabharata, the, 18, 128, 167, 175
Mahayana (Greater Vehicle), 17, 18, 20, 128
Maize, 139, 150, 151, 69
Makassar, 39, 41, 43, 44, 48, 185
Makassarese-Buginese, 11
Malacca, 26, 27, 37, 38, 39, 41, 42, 43, 44, 19; Strait of, 75
Malagassi language, 10
Malaya, 152, 199
Malay immigrants, 10
Malay language, 10, 92, 95, 167, 168
Malay-Polynesians, 9
Malays, 10, 134, 166, 206
Malaysia, 12, 156, 199, 200, 201, 202, 204, 206, 207, 208
Malaysian Borneo, 202
Malayu (Northern Kingdom of Sumatra), 19, 21
Manganese, 142
Mangkunegara lands, 50, 51

'Maphilindo', 200
Marshall Plan, the, 144
Marxist influence, 93, 94, 97, 50
Masjumi Party, 131, 181, 182, 183, 184, 185, 186, 187, 190, 191, 193, 195, 199
Mataram dynasty, 20, 21, 39, 40, 41, 44, 45, 46, 47, 48, 49, 50
Mecca, reform movements in, 129
Mechanization, 99
Medan, 124
Melanesian people, 9
Menangkabau, 11, 100, 130, 135, 136, 181
Mesolithic culture, 9
Middle class, the, 123–4
Middle East, the, 128
Mikoyan, Anastas, 202
Ming dynasty, 26
Mining Law (1899), 74
Ministry for Religious Affairs, 197
Minto, Lord, 62
Missionary schools, 80
Modernist Islam, 129, 131, 135, 136
Moluccas, the, 11, 13, 15, 21, 26, 27, 28, 39, 40, 42, 43, 49, 71, 145, 166, 180
Mongols, the, 26
Mook, H. V. Van (*see* Who's Who: p. 228), 108
Muhammad, the Prophet, 129, 170, 17
Muhammadiyah, the, 92, 131
'Multatuli' (*see* Dekker, Douwes)
Music, 166, 169–70, 172, 175
Muslims, 26, 37, 106, 128–31, 136, 137
'Mutual Help' Parliament, 195
Muzakkar, Kahar, 185, 205

NAGAPATAM, 20
Nahdatul Ulama (NU) Party, 131, 182, 183, 184, 186, 197
Nalanda (Buddhist university), 20
Nasution, General (*see* Who's Who: p. 228–9), 201, 202, 206
National Indies Party, the, 93, 94, 96
Nationalist Committee, the, 107
Nationalist Party, 107, 197
Natsir, Mohammed (*see* Who's Who: p. 229), 182, 192

237